W9-AXS-728

Quick Reference Guide™

Windows® 95

Karl Schwartz & Joanne Schwartz

14 East 38 St New York, NY 10016

First DDC Publishing, Inc. Printing

10   9   8   7   6   5   4   3   2

Catalog No. G6

ISBN: 1-56243-232-X

Printed in the United States of America

Introduction

The *DDC Quick Reference Guide for Microsoft®
Windows™ 95* will save you hours of searching through
technical manuals for directions.

In this guide you will find:

- Step-by-step instructions showing you how to perform
  Windows actions easily using a mouse — we explain basic
  mouse operations on page 25.

- Procedures that include the graphic controls and symbols
  appearing on your Windows screen.

- Topics grouped so related information is easy to find.
  (See the Table of Contents on the next page.)

We are confident our guide will help you to master and enjoy
Microsoft Windows 95.

Karl Schwartz and Joanne Schwartz

Assistant Editor . . . . *Rebecca Fiala*

Managing Editor . . . . *Kathy Berkemeyer*

Design and Layout . . . . . *Karl Schwartz and Joanne Schwartz*

*The end-user information in this book is based on information on
Windows 95 made public by Microsoft as of July 11, 1995.*

ii

Table of Contents

The Desktop

After starting Windows 95, you will see the **desktop** — the background area of your screen. The desktop is a **root folder** *(see Folders and Files on the next page)* from which all the items in your computer can be accessed. You can customize the desktop by placing your folders, files and shortcuts on it. **Permanent folders** such as My Computer and Recycle Bin appear as icons on the desktop. Network Neighborhood also appears if you are connected to a network.

At the bottom of the desktop is the **taskbar**. The taskbar contains the Start button and a clock. Buttons appear on the taskbar for each application and folder you open. The items introduced here are discussed on the pages that follow.

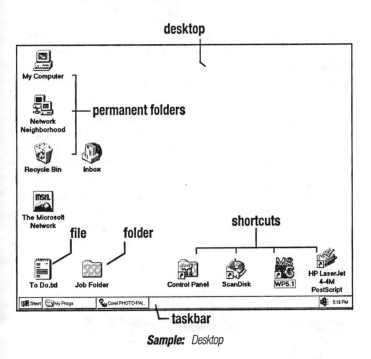

Sample: *Desktop*

2

Folders and Files

Folders store related items such as files and other folders. In previous versions of Windows, folders were called *directories*. The following are permanent folders that Windows maintains:

- Desktop — a root folder from which all other folders can be accessed.
- My Computer — contains your computer's drive icons, and the Control Panel, Printers and Dial-Up Networking folders.
- Recycle Bin — stores the files and folders you delete.

Files store data or programs, for example:

- Applications — program files that perform tasks.
- Data files — documents you create with an application.
- Shortcuts — files containing links to other items.

Icons represent closed files and folders. When you double-click an icon, such as the Art folder illustrated below, a folder **window** will open displaying its contents.

Naming files and file locations (paths) is easier in these ways:

- File names may contain spaces and can be as long as 255 characters. They cannot contain the following characters: \ * ? " < > | Windows creates an **alias** for each long file name so programs written prior to Windows 95 can read the new files. For example the file name MY FIRST DRAFT.TXT would appear as MYFIRS~1.TXT in these programs.
- You can use **Universal Naming Convention** (UNC) **pathnames** to identify the location of files on other computers as in this example: "\\Computername\sharename\file name"
  NOTE: Paths containing spaces require double quotes (").

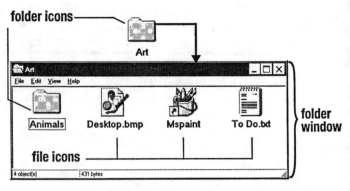

Sample: *Folders and Files*

My Computer

My Computer is a desktop folder containing **drive icons** and two permanent folders, **Control Panel** and **Printers**. The drive icons represent all the drives your computer is connected to, including **mapped network drives**. Mapped network drives are shared folders on other computers to which you have assigned a drive letter.

When you open a drive folder, it shows the files and folders contained in that drive.

The **Dial-Up Networking** folder also appears if you added this feature. Dial-Up Networking lets you extend your computer to include computers at remote sites.

How you will use My Computer: Typically, you will open My Computer to browse the drives connected to your computer.

You can access the My Computer folder in the following ways:

- **From the desktop** by double-clicking the *My Computer* icon.
- **From any folder window** by selecting it from the hierarchy of folders in the *Go to a different folder* list box on a folder's toolbar.
- **From Explorer** by selecting it from the hierarchy of folders in the *All Folders* pane.
- **From a common dialog box** by selecting it in the *Look in* list box.

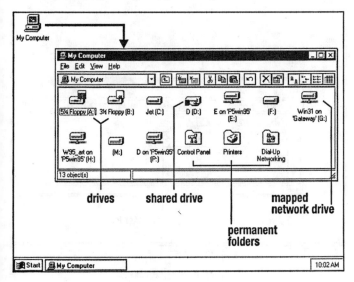

Sample: *My Computer*

Network Neighborhood

Network Neighborhood is a desktop folder that appears if your computer is connected to a network. This folder contains **computer icons** and the **Entire Network** permanent folder. The computer icons represent all the active computers in the current workgroup or domain.

When you open a computer folder, Windows displays the computer's shared resources, such as folders and printers. You can open the Entire Network folder to show all the domains and workgroups to which your computer is connected.

How you will use Network Neighborhood: Typically, you will open Network Neighborhood to browse the shared resources on other computers.

You can access the Network Neighborhood folder in the following ways:

- **From the desktop** by double-clicking the *Network Neighborhood* icon.
- **From any folder window** by selecting it from the hierarchy of folders in the *Go to a different folder* list box on a folder's toolbar.
- **From Explorer** by selecting it from the hierarchy of folders in the *All Folders* pane.
- **From a common dialog box** by selecting it in the *Look in* list box.

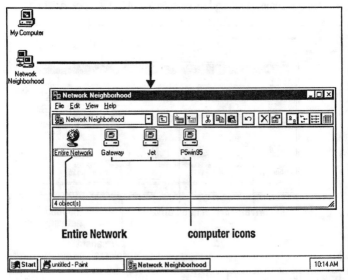

Sample: *Network Neighborhood*

Recycle Bin

Recycle Bin is a desktop folder in which Windows stores the items you delete. You can use Recycle Bin commands to return selected items to their original locations or permanently delete them. Windows automatically removes items from the Recycle Bin when they take up a specified percentage of available hard disk space.

NOTE: Files deleted from removable disks, such as floppy disks, and files deleted from within an application, are not placed in the Recycle Bin.

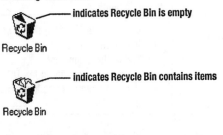

Drag items onto Recycle Bin to delete them ...

... then remove deleted items permanently or return selected items to their original locations.

Sample: *Recycle Bin*

The appearance of the Recycle Bin icon tells you about its contents as shown in the following illustration:

indicates Recycle Bin is empty

Recycle Bin

indicates Recycle Bin contains items

Recycle Bin

The Taskbar

Start button   **application and folder buttons**   **clock**

| Start | untitled - Paint | C:\Art | | 4:49 PM |

Sample: *Taskbar*

The illustration above shows the following taskbar controls:

Buttons on taskbar: Represent running applications and open folders. Click the button to switch to the application or folder window. Rest the pointer on a button to display its full name.

Clock area on taskbar: Double-click it to set the time or date quickly. Rest pointer on the clock to show the time and date. You can double-click icons for active devices (such as a printer or modem) that appear in this area to open them.

Start button: Click it to access the following:

Start menu items	Description
Programs	Point to this item to access the folders and applications it contains.
Documents	Point to this item to access recently opened documents.
Settings	Point to this item to access the Control Panel folder, Printers folder and taskbar properties.
Find	Point to this item to access the following Find options: Files or Folders, Computer or On The Microsoft Network.
Help	Click to open online Help for Windows.
Run...	Click to open an application, data file or folder by typing its name.
Shut Down...	Click to select the following shutdown options: • Shut down the computer? • Restart the computer? • Restart the computer in MS-DOS mode? • Close all programs and log on as a different user?

Shortcuts

Shortcuts are links to items you use often, such as applications, computers, documents, folders, printers, and shared items on other computers. Instead of browsing folders or menus each time you want to open an item, you can create a shortcut to that item and place it on the desktop or in a folder. Shortcut icons always have a **jump arrow** in the lower-left corner, as in these examples:

Floppy (B)   Wp.exe   Network   Notepad   Documents   HP printer   Control Panel

Shortcuts provide the following services and advantages:

Convenient copy and move: You can create a shortcut to a folder to which you often copy or move files. You can then drag files onto the shortcut to copy or move them to that folder.

Safety: You can delete a shortcut without deleting the item to which it is linked.

Flexibility: If the name or location of the item the shortcut is linked to changes, the shortcut will still work.

Convenient printing: Instead of opening a document and its application to print it, you can drag a document onto a printer shortcut.

About shortcuts and the Start menu: When you click the Start button, Windows opens the Start menu. The programs appearing in the Start and Programs menus are shortcuts to applications or documents. Windows stores these shortcuts in the Start Menu and Programs folders. You can open these folders and add or remove shortcuts to change what appears on the Start menu.

About shortcuts and the Send To command: When you right-click a file, Windows opens a shortcut menu displaying the Send To command. The items appearing on the Send To menu are shortcuts to destinations, such as disk drives, printers, faxes and folders. Windows stores these shortcuts in the SendTo folder. You can open the SendTo folder and add or remove the shortcuts to change what appears on the Send To menu.

Explorer

Explorer is an application that lets you browse, manage and use all the items in your computer. The Explorer window is divided into the **All Folders** pane on the left and the **Contents** pane on the right. You can size the panes by dragging the **split bar**.

In the All Folders pane:

- The desktop is the **root folder** from which all other folders can be accessed. Explorer shows the hierarchy of your folders below the Desktop folder.

- A ⊞ (plus sign) next to a folder indicates you can **expand** it to show its subfolders.

- A ⊟ (minus sign) next to a folder indicates you can **collapse** it to hide its subfolders.

In the Contents pane:

- Explorer shows the contents of the **selected folder**.

In the illustration, Large Icons is the **selected toolbar button**. This sets the display of items in the Contents pane.

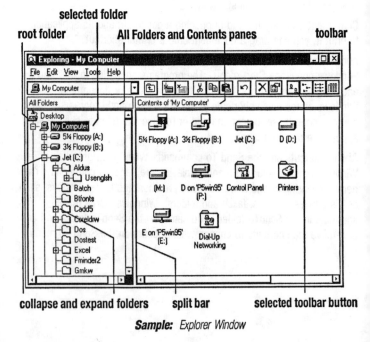

Sample: *Explorer Window*

Common Folder Toolbar

Folder windows and Explorer contain a **common toolbar**. This toolbar contains buttons (tools) to help you work with files and folders.
To display the toolbar, select Toolbar on the View menu from any folder window or while working with Explorer.

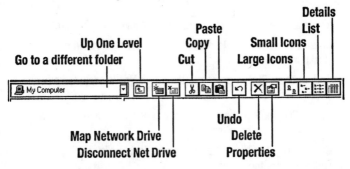

Toolbar items	Click to
Go to a different folder	Select a different folder from a hierarchy of folders.
Up One Level	Open parent folder of current folder.
Map Network Drive	Assign a drive letter to network drive or folder.
Disconnect Net Drive	Remove a mapped network connection.
Cut	Move selected items to the Clipboard.
Copy	Copy selected items to the Clipboard.
Paste	Insert contents of Clipboard.
Undo	Cancel last action.
Delete	Delete selected items.
Properties	Show or change properties of selected item.
Large Icons	Show contents as large icons.
Small Icons	Show contents as small icons.
List	Show contents in a list.
Details	Show details of contents such as file size.

Window Controls

The illustration below shows the following window controls:

Close button: Click it to close the window.

Control symbol: Click it to open a menu containing commands to control the window.

Maximize button: Click it to enlarge the window to fill the screen.

Minimize button: Click it to reduce the window to a button on the taskbar.

Restore button: Click it to restore the maximized window to its previous size.

Taskbar: Click buttons on it to select a window that is not in view or open a window you have minimized.

Title bar: Drag it to move the window, or double-click it to maximize/restore the window.

Window border or corner: Drag it to change the size of the window.

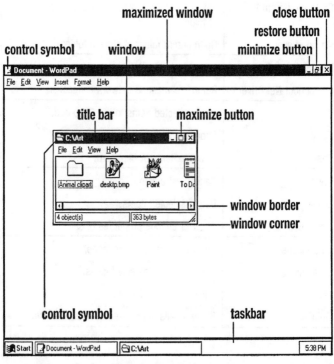

Sample: *Window Controls*

Dialog Box Controls

When a Windows application needs information from the user, a dialog box appears. Dialog boxes may contain the following:

Control	Example	Description
check box	☐ ☑	Provides for the selection or deselection of an option. A selected check box contains a check mark. More than one check box may be selected at a time.
command button	OK	Carries out actions described in the button's name.
drop-down list box		Provides for the selection of an item in a list that opens when you click the drop-down list arrow. The currently selected list item is displayed in the box.
increment box		Provides a space for typing a value. Up and down arrows give you a way to select a value with the mouse.
list box		Displays a list of items from which selections can be made. A list box may have a scroll bar that can be used to show hidden items.
option button	○ ◉	Provides for the selection of one option in a group. A selected option button contains a dot.
scroll bar		Provides scroll arrows and a scroll box on a horizontal or vertical bar that you can use to show hidden items in a list.
text box		Provides a space for typing in information.

Common Dialog Boxes

Windows 95 uses **common dialog boxes** to help you locate, select, save and open files on local and network drives. In these dialog boxes, you can also perform many file management tasks (such as create a folder, copy, move and delete) by right-clicking or dragging the items it displays. The illustration below shows the following controls:

Look in list box: Shows the current folder. Click to select a different folder from the hierarchy of folders in your computer.

List of items: Shows the contents of the current folder. You can double-click an item in this list to open it.

List and Details buttons: Click to change the view of items in the list.

Up One Level button: Click to select the parent of the current folder.

File name text box: Type a file name pattern with wildcards (e.g., *.bmp) in this box. This limits the files displayed in the list of items. You can also enter the file name you want to open in this box.

Files of type list box: Click to select a file type to display in the list.

Open button: Click to open the selected item in the list.

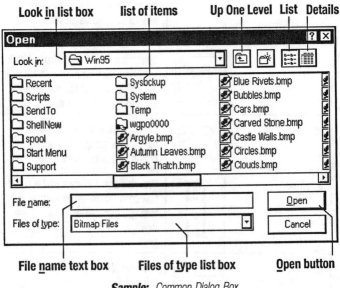

Sample: *Common Dialog Box*

The Find Command

As computer systems and networks get larger, the problem of finding files becomes more complex and difficult. The Find command on the Start menu helps you solve this problem. The illustration below shows the following Find dialog box controls:

Named text box: Type part or all of the name for the items to find.

Look in list box: Select or type a place to search. You can select My Computer in this box to search your entire system.

Tabs: Click to set other criteria for search.

Command buttons: Click to start, stop or perform a new search.

Result list: Found items appear in the result list. You can work with these items in many ways. For example, you can right-drag a found item onto the desktop to create a shortcut for the item.

You can save search (settings/results) using Find menu commands.

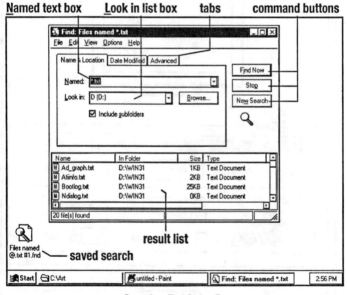

Sample: Find Dialog Box

Properties

Properties describe an item's characteristics and settings. For example, the properties of a file include its name and size; the properties of a disk include its used space, free space and capacity.

Everything in Windows 95 has properties that you can view or change. To view or set an item's properties, right-click the item, then click Properties on the shortcut menu that appears. The illustration below shows the properties of a computer's display. To access your computer's display properties, right-click an empty area of the desktop.

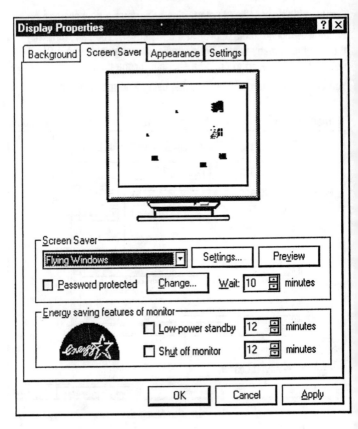

Sample: *Screen Saver Tab in Display Properties Dialog Box*

Sharing Data Using the Clipboard

When you cut or copy selected data in an application[1] Windows sends
the data to the **Clipboard** — a temporary storage area[2] You can then
paste the data from the Clipboard into a document[3] You can view data
in the Clipboard with the **Clipboard Viewer** program. You can transfer
text and graphic data between applications in this way.

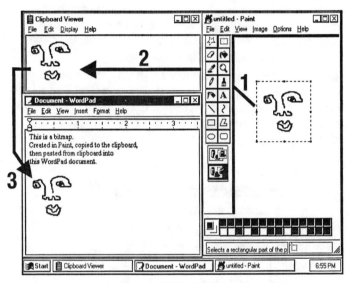

Sample: *Data Copied to the Clipboard and Pasted into a Document*

Inserting OLE Objects in Documents

Windows supports **Object Linking and Embedding** (OLE). This lets you insert embedded or linked objects into a document. An **object** is a collection of information created with an OLE **object application**, such as Paint. A **container application** is one that can receive OLE objects, such as WordPad.

Embedded objects: When you insert an embedded object, Windows inserts the object *as a copy* in the document. You can edit the embedded object in-place from within the document. This means the object application menus and tools replace the container application menu and tools while you edit the object.

Link objects: When you insert a linked object, Windows inserts a *connection to the object* in the document. You can edit a linked object from any document that has received the object. When you edit a linked object, all other documents with links to that object are updated automatically.

object application menus and tools

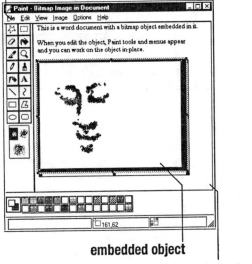

embedded object

document workspace

Sample: *Editing Embedded Object In-Place*

MS-DOS Applications

Windows 95 provides more flexibility and greater performance for your MS-DOS applications or when working from the MS-DOS prompt.

More window sizes and fonts: When running your MS-DOS applications in a window, you can select more window and font sizes. If you decide to show the toolbar, you can quickly change font sizes as you work in the window. You can run your MS-DOS applications full-screen or in a window.

Setting properties is easier: Editing a PIF file is no longer required. When you want to customize the settings for an MS-DOS application, just right-click the title bar and select Properties from the shortcut menu. Then, set the desired properties on the property sheets.

More conventional memory: Windows' new system architecture frees more conventional memory for use by your MS-DOS applications.

MS-DOS mode: This property sets an MS-DOS application to use all system resources. When you select this mode, your computer will restart and run only the application. When you quit the application, Windows will restart automatically. This option is useful for resource-hungry applications, such as games, that cannot run otherwise.

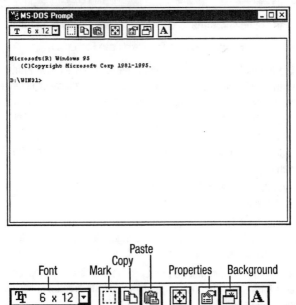

Sample: *MS-DOS Session and Toolbar*

Windows Printing

In Windows 95, printing is easier to set up — faster and more flexible than previous versions of Windows.

Printers folder   **print queue**

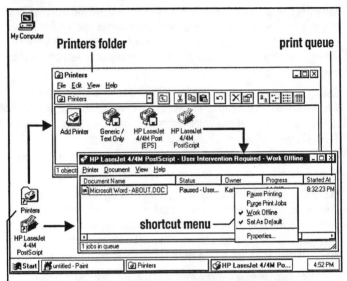

shortcut menu

You can create shortcuts to the Printers folder and a print queue.

Sample: *Printers Folder and Open Print Queue*

The Add Printer Wizard: The Printers folder contains the Add Printer Wizard that will walk you through the steps to add a local or network printer. Windows stores printers in the Printers folder. You can print from any Windows application to the printers you add to Windows.

Easy network printer setup: Browse computers in the Network Neighborhood, then select a shared printer and click Install on the File menu.

Drag and drop printing: You can drag a file onto a printer icon or printer shortcut to print it.

Print using Send To command: You can add a shortcut to a printer in the SendTo folder. Then, to print a file, right-click it and point to Send To. Next, click the printer shortcut.

Offline printing: You can set a printer to work offline. This option is available for network printers or printers added to a portable computer. Windows stores the documents you print to the offline printer in a local print queue until your computer has access to the printer.

Continued ...

Windows Printing (continued)

View and manage print jobs: Double-click the printer icon or printer shortcut to view documents printing on it. You can then cancel, pause or change the order of print jobs in the print queue.

Print settings: You can change print settings for a single document from your application (select Page Setup or similar command), or you can set the default properties for a printer from the Start menu (Start, Settings, Printers). Then, right-click the printer and click Properties from the shortcut menu.

Windows Fonts

The Windows Fonts folder lets you add and remove TrueType fonts. You can print using any font stored in the Fonts folder from any Windows application. The Fonts folder is located in the Control Panel.

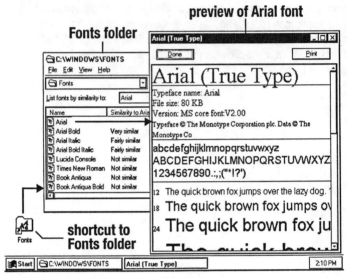

Sample: Fonts Folder and Previewed Font

Adding fonts: From the Fonts folder, select Install New Font from the File menu.

Remove fonts: From the Fonts folder, select fonts to delete, then select Delete from the File menu.

Special characters: The Character Map application lets you select special characters in the installed font families and paste them into your Windows applications.

List and preview fonts: The Fonts folder provides commands to list fonts by similarity; you can double-click any font to preview it.

Display fonts: You can use installed fonts to set display properties of text items in Windows.

Windows Networking

Windows' built-in networking lets you share data and computer resources (folders and printers) with other computers in your workgroup or network domain.

You can use the following features to work with network resources:

- Any folder's **Go to a different folder drop-down list** to select a network folder to which you are already connected.

- Any folder's **Map Network Drive button** (on toolbar) to connect to a shared drive or folder on a network.

- Any folder's **Disconnect Net Drive button** (on toolbar) to disconnect from a shared drive on a network.

- The **Network Neighborhood folder** to browse computers and their resources on a network.

- The **Entire Network folder** (in Network Neighborhood) to view the structure of other network workgroups and domains.

- **Computer icons** (in Network Neighborhood) to use shared resources (drives, folders, printers) on computers to which you are connected.

- The **My Computer folder** (on desktop) to view all *mapped network drives* — network drives to which you have assigned drive letters.

- The **Microsoft Exchange application** to send and receive e-mail, faxes and documents to/from users on other computers.

- The **Dial-Up Networking application** (in My Computer) to connect to other remote computers via modem.

Sample: *Accessing Network Neighborhood from My Computer Folder*

Windows Security

Windows lets you protect resources you have shared with others on a network. This is a list of terms and features related to Windows security:

Log on security: A kind of security in which Windows requires each user to enter a user name and password before giving the user access to the network. This establishes a Master Key password *(see below)* that can be passed to other programs requiring passwords.

Master Key password: A password associated with a user name that is set when a user first logs on. You can change the Master Key password with the Password tool in the Control Panel.

Password cache: A feature that saves the password used when you connect to a secured resource for the first time. The user need only log on using the same user name and password (Master Key) to connect to the same resource because the password is then supplied by the password cache.

Master Key: A password associated with a user name that's established when a user first logs on. The Master Key can speed access to other programs and resources:

- It can be passed to other programs that require passwords, such as Microsoft Exchange.

- It enables the user's password cache *(see above)*, which makes it easier to reconnect to shared resources that require passwords.

Local security: A type of security relating to resources on a single computer that's operated by multiple users.

Network security: A type of security relating to shared resources on a computer to which others may connect through a network. Windows provides two kinds of network security:

- **Share level security** — this lets you specify a password for each resource you share.

- **User-level security** — this lets you specify users and groups that can have access to the resources you share based on a Windows NT domain, a Windows NT Advanced Server, or a Novell NetWare server.

Sharing: An action specifying how an item can by used by others. For example, you can specify that a directory be shared and that its share name and its access type is read-only. You can also set passwords for a shared directory. The method of sharing depends on the kind of network security, however.

Windows Applications

Windows 95 comes with an array of applications that can help you to manage your system and do your work.

Application	Lets you
Briefcase	Synchronize files you work with on different computers.
Calculator	Perform standard and advanced calculations.
CD Player	Play audio compact discs.
Character Map	Select and insert special characters into any Windows document.
Clipboard Viewer	View data stored in the Clipboard.
Dial-Up Networking	Connect to local and network resources on a remote computer that is running dial-up server software.
Direct Cable Connection	Connect to the local and network resources on a Windows 95 computer that is also running Direct Cable Connection.
Disk Defragmenter	Move fragmented files so they are stored contiguously (in one piece) on a disk.
DriveSpace	Compress files on a disk and provides commands to manage compressed disks.
HyperTerminal	Connect to a remote computer for the purpose of exchanging information and files.
Media Player	Play multimedia files, such as video files and compact discs.
Microsoft Backup	Back up files to a local, network or tape drive.
Microsoft Exchange	Send, receive and manage electronic messages and faxes from one location.
Microsoft Fax	Compose, address and send fax messages.

Continued ...

Windows Applications (continued)

Application	Lets you
Net Watcher	Monitor, manage and create network shares on your computer and administer network shares on a remote computer.
Notepad	Create and edit text files.
Paint	Create and edit bitmap drawings.
Phone Dialer	Record and dial phone numbers from your computer.
ScanDisk	Scan and fix errors found on disks.
Sound Recorder	Record, play back and edit sounds.
The Microsoft Network	Access Microsoft's online information service.
Volume Control	Control the audio volume for playback, recording and other installed audio devices.
WordPad	Create, edit, format and print documents.

Mouse Procedures

*NOTE: Procedures in this book use the left button as the primary mouse button. You can change the button configuration for your mouse from left-handed to right-handed, however. See **Set Mouse Properties**, page 177.*

Point to an Item

• Move mouse until ⇖ (pointer) is in contact with desired item.

NOTE: The pointer is an arrow-shaped graphic that moves as you move the mouse. The shape of the pointer changes depending on the object it is pointing to and the kinds of actions it can do.

Click an Item

1 Point to item.

2 Quickly press and release *left* mouse button.

Double-click an Item

1 Point to item.

2 Press and release *left* mouse button *twice* in rapid succession.

Drag an Item

1 Point to item.

2 Press and hold *left* mouse button while moving mouse.

3 Release mouse button to complete the action.

Right-click an Item (Open Shortcut Menu)

1 Point to item.

2 Press and release *right* mouse button.

3 Select desired option from shortcut menu.

Right-drag an Item

1 Point to item.

2 Press and hold *right* mouse button while moving mouse.

3 Release mouse button.

4 Select desired option from menu that appears.

Select Item from Start Menu

The Start menu lets you perform common tasks like starting programs, opening documents and shutting down your computer.

1 Click . . . . | 🏁 **Start** |
on taskbar.

To open a submenu.

- Point to . . . . *menu item with* ▸
   NOTE: You can open submenus in this way until
   you see the item you want to select.

2 Click . . . . *desired menu item*

NOTE: Menu items may contain the following indicators:

   ▸   *A triangle indicates a submenu will open.*

   ...   *An ellipsis indicates another window or*
   dialog box will open.

Start menu steps will be shown as:

1 Click . . . . | 🏁 **Start** |
2 Point to . . . . *menu item* ▸
OR
   Click . . . . *menu item*

Select Item from a Menu Bar

Most Windows applications contain a menu bar located just below the application window title bar. Each name on the menu bar contains a set of menu items.

1 Click . . . . *desired menu name*
on menu bar.

2 Point to or click . . . . *desired menu item*

Keyboard Shortcut:

1 Press . . . . **Alt** + *underlined letter*
in menu name.

2 Press . . . . *underlined letter*
in menu item.

NOTE: *Menu items may contain the following indicators:*

▶   *A triangle indicates a submenu will open.*

...   *An ellipsis indicates another window or dialog box will open.*

key   *A key name (such as Del) shows a fast way to perform the action without opening the menu.*

✓   *A check mark indicates the item is selected.*

●   *A circle indicates the selected item is in a list in which only one item can be selected.*

Menu bar steps will be shown as:

1 Click . . . . *menu name*

2 Point to . . . . *menu item* ▶

OR

Click . . . . *menu item*

Select Item from a Shortcut Menu

You can right-click many items to open a shortcut menu containing commands that pertain to the item.

1 Right–click . . . . **desired item**

2 Click . . . . **desired menu item**

> NOTE: *Menu items may contain the following indicators:*
>
> ▶   *A triangle indicates submenu will open.*
>
> ...   *An ellipsis indicates another window or dialog box will open.*

Shortcut menu steps will be shown as:

1 Right–click . . . . *item*

2 Point to . . . . *menu item* ▶

OR

Click . . . . *menu item*

Select Options in a Dialog Box

Select a Tab

Some dialog boxes include tabs that group related options.

• Click . . . . **tab name**

Selected tabs show related options in dialog box.

Selected tabs will be shown as:

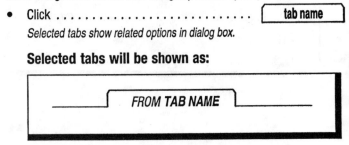

FROM TAB NAME

Continued ...

Select Options in a Dialog Box (continued)

Select Item in a Drop-Down List

1 Click drop-down list arrow . . . .

   If item is not in view:

   • Click scroll arrows . . . .

2 Click . . . . ***item***
Selected item appears in the closed list.

   Drop-down list steps will be shown as:

> • Select item in . . . . ***list name:***

Select One Item in a List Box

   If item is not in view:

   • Click scroll arrows . . . .

• Click . . . . ***item***
Selected item is highlighted.

Select Consecutive Items in a List Box

1 Click . . . . ***first item***

2 Press and hold **Shift** while clicking . . . . . . ***last item in group***
Selected items are highlighted.

Select Multiple Items in a List Box

• Press and hold **Ctrl** while clicking . . . . ***each item***
Selected items are highlighted.

   List box steps will be shown as:

> • Select item(s) in . . . . ***list name:*** list box

Continued ...

Select Options in a Dialog Box (continued)

Type Data in an Empty Text Box

1 Click anywhere in text box . . . .

2 Type the data . . . . *data*

Replace Data in a Text Box

1 Double-click data to replace in text box . . . . `data`
Existing data is highlighted.

2 Type new data . . . . *new data*

Edit Data in a Text Box

1 Click desired character position in text box . . . . `data`

If editing is required:

- Press . . . . `Del`
to remove characters to the right.

 OR

 Press . . . . `BkSp`
 to remove characters to the left.

2 Type new data . . . . *new data*

 Text box steps will be shown as:

> - Type information in . . . . . . *text box name:*

Select/Deselect a Check Box

- Click . . . . ☐ *option name*
to select it.

 OR

 Click . . . . ☑ *option name*
 to deselect it.
 NOTE: More than one check box may be selected in a group.

 Check box steps will be shown as:

> - Select or deselect . . . . ☐ *option name*

Continued ...

Select Options in a Dialog Box (continued)

Select an Option Button

- Click . . . . $\bigcirc$ *option name*
  to select it.
  NOTE: Only one option button may be selected in a group.

Option button steps will be shown as:

> - Select . . . . $\bigcirc$ *option name*

Select a Command Button

- Click . . . . | command name |
  A selected command button carries out the command action.

Command button steps will be shown as:

> - Click . . . . | command name |

Specify a Value in an Increment Box

1 Click in . . . . ⬍

2 Type desired value . . . . *number*
  OR
  Click up or down increment arrows . . . . ⬍
  The typed or selected value appears in the box.

Increment box steps will be shown as:

> - Type or select
>   value in . . . . *increment box name:* ⬍

Get Help in a Dialog Box

1   Click Help button . . . .   🔲**?**

2   Click . . . .   ***dialog box option***
    Windows displays help for the item.

Open Windows 95 Help

1   Click . . . .   ⊞ Start

2   Click . . . .   📙 <u>H</u>elp

    Windows displays Help Topics: Windows Help dialog box.

3   Select the desired tab and follow the prompts.

Move a Window

By Dragging

•   Drag window's . . . .   Title bar
    to new location.

Using Taskbar

NOTE: *This method is useful when the title bar of the window you want to move is off the screen.*

1   Right-click . . . . ***folder or application button on taskbar***
    to move.

2   Click . . . .   <u>M</u>ove

3   Press . . . .   ⬍
    until the window is positioned as desired.

4   Press . . . .   ⏎
    to end moving.

Move an Icon

- Drag . . . . *icon*
  to new location.

Change Size of a Window

*NOTE: A maximized window must be restored (page 36) before you
can size it.*

By Dragging

1 Point to . . . . *border or corner of window*
to size.
Pointer becomes one of the following: ←→ ↖ ↘

2 Drag . . . . *window outline*
to desired size.

3 Repeat steps above until desired size is obtained.

Using Taskbar

1 Right-click . . . . *folder or application button on taskbar*
to size.

2 Click . . . . **Size**

3 Press . . . . 🔼🔽
once, in direction of border to change.

4 Press . . . . 🔼🔽
until the window's border is the desired size.

5 Press . . . . ↵
to end sizing.

Minimize a Window

Reduces folder and application windows to buttons on the taskbar; reduces document windows to buttons in the application workspace.

Using Minimize Button

- Click window's **minimize** button . . . . **▬**

Using Control Symbol

1 Click window's . . . . *control symbol*

> NOTE: *The control symbol of a maximized folder or application window is located to the left of its title bar. The control symbol of a maximized document window is located to the left of the application menu bar.*

2 Click . . . . **Minimize**

Using Taskbar

1 Right-click . . . . *folder or application button on taskbar* to minimize.

2 Click . . . . **Minimize**

All Windows Using Taskbar

1 Right-click empty area on . . . . *taskbar*

2 Click . . . . **Minimize All Windows**

Maximize a Window

Expands folder and application windows to fill the desktop; document windows fill the application workspace. After maximizing a window, the restore button appears.

Using Maximize Button

• Click window's **maximize** button . . . . □

Using Control Symbol

1 Click window's . . . . *control symbol* on left side of title bar.

2 Click . . . . **Maximize**

Using Title Bar

• Double-click window's . . . . ▬ Title bar

Using Taskbar

1 Right-click . . . . *folder or application button on taskbar*

2 Click . . . . **Maximize** to maximize.

Restore a Maximized Window

*Restores a maximized window to its previous size. After restoring a window,
the maximize button appears.*

Using Restore Button

- Click window's **restore** button . . . . ▣

Using Control Symbol

1 Click window's . . . . *control symbol*

   NOTE: *The control symbol of a maximized folder or
   application window is located to the left of its title bar.
   The control symbol of a maximized document window
   is located to the left of the application menu bar.*

2 Click . . . . **Restore**

Using Title Bar

- Double-click window's . . . . [*Title bar*]

Using Taskbar

1 Right-click . . . . *folder or application button on taskbar*
   to restore.

2 Click . . . . **Restore**

Close a Window

Using Close Button

- Click window's **close** button . . . . ☒

Using Control Symbol

1 Click window's . . . . *control symbol*

  NOTE: *The control symbol of a maximized folder or*
  application window is located to the left of its title bar.
  The control symbol of a maximized document window
  is located to the left of the application menu bar.

2 Click . . . . **Close**

Using Keyboard

NOTE: *Closes application and folder windows — not document windows.*

- Press . . . . **Alt** + **F4**

Using Taskbar

1 Right-click . . . . *folder or application button on taskbar*
  to close.

2 Click . . . . **Close**

Arrange Open Windows on Desktop

- Right-click any blank area on . . . . *taskbar*

  ### In Overlapping Order

  - Click . . . . **Cascade**

  ### Evenly from Top to Bottom

  - Click . . . . **Tile Horizontally**

  ### Evenly from Left to Right

  - Click . . . . **Tile Vertically**

Scroll

Moves an area of hidden data into view.

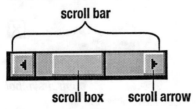

Using Scroll Arrows

*   Click . . . . **left or right scroll arrow**
    to scroll horizontally in small steps through list or workspace.

    OR

    Click . . . . **up or down scroll arrow**
    to scroll vertically in small steps through list or workspace.

Using Scroll Box

*   Drag . . . . **horizontal scroll box**
    to scroll horizontally to any position in list or workspace.

    OR

    Drag . . . . **vertical scroll box**
    to scroll vertically to any position in list or workspace.

Using Scroll Bar

*   Click . . . . **vertical scroll bar**
    above or below scroll box to move vertically to previous or next
    area in list or workspace.

    OR

    Click . . . . **horizontal scroll bar**
    to right or left of scroll box to move horizontally to previous or
    next area in list or workspace.

Undo Last Command to Arrange Windows on Desktop

1 Right-click any blank area on . . . . *taskbar*

2 Click . . . . **U**ndo . . .

Show Full Name of Item on Taskbar

- Point to . . . . *item on taskbar*

Start Windows Options

1 Turn your computer system on.

2 When **Starting Windows 95...** message appears,

Press . . . . `F8`

Windows displays the following options:

1. Normal

2. Logged (\BOOTLOG.TXT)

3. Safe mode

4. Safe mode with network support

5. Step-by-step confirmation

6. Command prompt only

7. Safe mode command prompt only

8. Previous version of MS-DOS

3 Press desired function keys.

F5=Safe mode Shift+F5=Command prompt Shift+F8=Step-by-step confirmation

AND/OR

Press . . . . *number*

(1–8) of desired option *(see above)*.

Set Display Background Properties

1   Right-click empty area on . . . . *desktop*

2   Click . . . . **P**roperties

> ## FROM BACKGROUND

To select a display pattern:

- Select desired pattern in . . . . **P**attern list box

To edit a pattern:

a   Select desired pattern in . . . . **P**attern list box

b   Click . . . . | **E**dit Pattern... |

c   Click in . . . . **P**attern display area
  to add or subtract elements.

To save changes to pattern:

- Click . . . . | **C**hange |

To save pattern with a new name:

1. Type name in . . . . **N**ame: | ▼ |

2. Click . . . . | **A**dd |

d   Click . . . . | **D**one |

To select a wallpaper display:

- Select desired wallpaper in . . . . **W**allpaper list box

  OR

  a   Click . . . . | **B**rowse... |

  b   Select desired bitmap file.

  c   Click . . . . | OK |

Continued ...

Set Display Background Properties (continued)

To set placement of wallpaper:

- Select .... ○ **T**ile

  OR

  Select .... ○ **C**enter

3 Click .... Apply

to apply changes and remain in dialog box.

OR

Click .... OK

to apply changes and exit dialog box.

Set Screen Saver Properties

1 Right-click empty area on .... *desktop*

2 Click .... **P**roperties

FROM SCREEN SAVER

To select a screen saver:

- Select desired screen
  saver in .... **S**creen Saver [▾]

To set options for selected screen saver:

a Click .... Se**t**tings...

b Select desired screen saver options.

c Click .... OK

To preview screen saver:

a Click .... Pre**v**iew

b Move mouse to end preview.

Continued ...

Set Screen Saver Properties (continued)

To set screen saver wait time:

- Type or select time in . . . . <u>W</u>ait: [🔼🔽] minutes

To set password for screen saver:

a Select . . . . ☐ <u>P</u>assword protected

b Click . . . . [C<u>h</u>ange...]

c Type password in . . . . <u>N</u>ew password: [   ]

d Type password again in Con<u>f</u>irm new password: [   ]

e Click . . . . [OK   ]

To set energy savings features:

NOTE: These options may not be available for your display.

a Select . . . . ☐ <u>L</u>ow-power standby

b Type or select
time in . . . . <u>L</u>ow-power standby [🔼🔽] minutes

AND/OR

a Select . . . . ☐ Sh<u>u</u>t off monitor

b Type or select
time in . . . . Sh<u>u</u>t off monitor [🔼🔽] minutes

3 Click . . . . [Apply]
to apply changes and remain in dialog box.

OR

Click . . . . [OK   ]
to apply changes and exit dialog box.

Set Display Appearance Properties

1 Right-click empty area on .... *desktop*

2 Click .... **Properties**

FROM *APPEARANCE*

To select an appearance scheme:

- Select desired scheme in ...... **Scheme:** [_____ ▼]

To set attributes for display items:

a Select item to change in .... **Item:** [_____ ▼]

OR

Click item to change in .... *sample area*

b Select attribute(s) for selected item.

Items and attributes include:

3D Objects — color, font color

Active Title Bar — size, color, font, font size, font color and attributes

Active Window Border — size and color

Application Background — color

Caption Buttons — size

Desktop — color

Icon — size, font, font size, font attributes

Icon Spacing (Horizontal) — size

Icon Spacing (Vertical) — size

Icon Title

*Inactive Title Bar — size, color, font, font size, font color
    and attributes*

Inactive Window Border — size and color

Menu — size, color, font, font size, font color and attributes

Message Box — font, font size, font color and attributes

Palette Title — size, font, font size and attributes

Scrollbar — size

Selected Items — size, color, font, font size, font color and attributes

ToolTip — color, font, font size, font color and attributes

Window — color and font color

Continued ...

Set Display Appearance Properties (continued)

To save current appearance settings as a scheme:

a Click . . . . | Sa̲ve As... |

b Type name for scheme in . . . . | |

c Click . . . . | OK |

To delete an appearance scheme:

a Select desired scheme in . . . . . . **Scheme:** | ▼ |

b Click . . . . | De̲lete |

3 Click . . . . | Apply |
to apply changes and remain in dialog box.

OR

Click . . . . | OK |
to apply changes and exit dialog box.

Set Monitor Display Properties

NOTE: Options will depend on your monitor and adapter type.

1 Right-click empty area on . . . . ***desktop***

2 Click . . . . **P̲roperties**

⌐──── *FROM SETTINGS* ────⌐

To select a color palette:

• Select desired palette in . . . **C̲olor palette:** | ▼ |
NOTE: Options will depend on your monitor and adapter type.

To set display resolution:

• Drag ***slider*** in . . . . **D̲esktop area**
to set number of pixels to display.

Continued ...

Set Monitor Display Properties (continued)

To set font size Windows displays:

- Select font size in . . . . **F**ont size [　　　　] ▼

To set custom font size Windows displays:

a Click . . . . [C**u**stom...]

b Select percent of
normal in . . **S**cale fonts to be [　　　] ⬍ of normal size

OR

Drag any part of . . . . *ruler*
left or right to set a custom size.

c Click . . . . [OK]

To change display type:

a Click . . . . [Change Display **T**ype...]

Windows displays current adapter and monitor type.
CAUTION: Selecting the wrong adapter or monitor type
may cause your system to work improperly.

b Select the Change button for the item you want to change,
then carefully follow screen prompts.

*NOTE: You can change the **A**dapter Type or **M**onitor Type.*

3 Click . . . . [**A**pply]

to apply changes and remain in dialog box.

OR

Click . . . . [OK]

to apply changes and exit dialog box.

Set Taskbar Properties

1 Right-click empty area on . . . . *taskbar*

2 Click . . . . **P**r**operties**

> ### FROM TASKBAR OPTIONS

To change taskbar on-top setting:

● Select or deselect . . . . ☐ Always on **t**op

To reduce taskbar to a thin line:

● Select . . . . ☐ A**u**to hide

> NOTE: *Be sure to select* **Always on t**op *and* **A**u**to hide** *to*
> *ensure that the taskbar will be available, even*
> *when you maximize a Windows application.*

To change icon size of items on Start menu:

● Select or deselect. . . ☐ Show **s**mall icons in Start menu

To show or hide clock area:

● Select or deselect . . . . ☐ Show **C**lock

3 Click . . . . | OK |

Move Taskbar

1 Point to empty area on . . . . *taskbar*

2 Drag . . . . *pointer*
to left, right, top or bottom of desktop.

3 Release mouse button when taskbar appears in desired area.

Show Hidden Taskbar

● Point to . . . . *thin line*
on left, right, top or bottom of desktop.

Find Files and Folders

*Finds applications, data files, shortcuts, printers, and folders
on your computer, including network drives to which you have assigned
drive letters.*

1 **a** Click . . . . **Start**

    b Point to . . . . 🔍 **F**ind ▶

    c Click . . . . 📄 **F**iles or Folders...

OR   *— FROM EXPLORER WINDOW—*

    a Click . . . . **Tools**

    b Point to . . . . **F**ind ▶

    c Click . . . . **F**iles or Folders...

NOTE: *You can also right-click a folder you want to search,
then click **F**ind to search that folder.*

FROM NAME & LOCATION

2 Type or select file or folder name in . . **N**amed: `[          ▼]`

    NOTE: *You can include wildcards or type partial names,
or you can select past search items from the drop-down list.*

3 Type or select location to search in . . **L**ook in: `[          ▼]`

To exclude subfolders from search:

• Deselect . . . . ☑ Include **s**ubfolders

4 To set other criteria, see the following:
    ***Set Date Criteria for Find Command,** page 49.*
    ***Set Advanced Criteria for Find Command,** page 48.*

5 Click . . . . `Find Now`
    Found files appear in a result list.

To stop search:

• Click . . . . `Stop`

Continued ...

Find Files or Folders (continued)

To clear current results:

a Click .... | New Search |

b Click .... | OK |

NOTE: *You can work with found items in many ways. For example, you can open a found item by double-clicking it. See **Work with Found Files and Folders**, page 50.*

Set Advanced Criteria for Find Command

1   Follow steps to find files or folders (page 47).

> **FROM ADVANCED**

To set file type to find:

* Select file type in .... **Of type:** | ▼ |

To find files containing text:

a Type desired text in .... **Containing text:** | |

b Click .... **Options**
on menu bar.

c Select or deselect .... **Case Sensitive**

To set size criteria:

a Select At least or At most in ..... **Size is:** | ▼ |

b Type or select value in .... | ⬍ | **KB**

2   Set other criteria.

OR

Click .... | Find Now |
Found files appear in a result list.

Set Date Criteria for Find Command

1 Follow steps to find files or folders (page 47).

> **FROM DATE MODIFIED**

- Select .... ◯ **All files**

OR

To limit range to specific dates:

a Select .... ◯ **Find all files created or modified**

b Select .... ◯ **between**

c Type dates in ...... **between** [＿＿] and [＿＿]

To limit range to months:

a Select .... ◯ **Find all files created or modified**

b Select .... ◯ **during the previous**

c Type or select value in .... [＿＿ ⬍] **month(s)**

To limit range to days:

a Select .... ◯ **Find all files created or modified**

b Select .... ◯ **during the previous**

c Type or select value in .... [＿＿ ⬍] **day(s)**

2 Set other criteria.

OR

Click .... [Fi_nd Now]

Found files appear in a result list.

Work with Found Files and Folders

Windows displays found files and folders in a result list. The list is divided into the following columns: Name, In Folder, Size, Type and Modified.

Find Result List — Change Size

- Drag . . . . *border or corner*
  of Find window in direction to size.

Find Result List — Change Column Size

- Drag . . . . *right border*
  of column heading to size.

Find Result List — Sort

- Click . . . . *column heading*
  to sort by.
  NOTE: Click column heading again to switch between ascending and descending order for that column.

Find Result List — Menu Options

NOTE: Menu items will depend upon the items you select in the result list.

1 Select desired files and folders (page 64) in result list.

2 Click . . . . **File**
  File menu items may include: Create Shortcut, Delete, Edit, Explore, Find, Open Containing Folder, Open/Open With, Print, Properties, Quick View, Rename, Save Search, Send To, Sharing

OR

  Click . . . . **Edit**
  Edit menu items may include: Copy, Cut, Invert Selection, Select All, Undo

OR

  Click . . . . **View**
  View menu items may include: Large Icons, Small Icons, List, Details, Arrange Icons, Line up Icons

3 Click appropriate menu item.

Continued ...

Work with Found Files and Folders (continued)

Find Result List — Right-Click Options

1 Select desired files and folders (page 64) in result list.

2 Right-click . . . . *selection*
A shortcut menu appears.
NOTE: Items on menu depend upon selection in result list.

3 Click appropriate shortcut menu item.
Shortcut menu items may include: Copy, Create Shortcut, Cut, Delete,
Edit, Explore, Find, Open, Open With, Print, Properties, Quick View,
Rename, Send To, Sharing

Find Result List — Right-Drag Options

1 Select desired files and folders (page 64) in result list.

2 Right-drag . . . . *selection*
onto destination item.
A menu appears.

3 Click appropriate menu item.
Right-drag menu items may include: Copy Here, Create Shortcut(s)
Here, Move Here, Open With

Find Result List — Save Settings and/or Result List

1 Click . . . . **Options**

2 Select or deselect . . . . **Save Results**
Select to save search results in addition to your search criteria.

3 Click . . . . **File, Save Search**
Windows places a "Files named..." icon on the desktop. You can double-
click this icon to perform the search again, and/or view the results if you
selected the **Save Results** option.

Open Files and Folders

*Opens files or folders from the **desktop**, a **folder window**, the **Explorer** Contents pane, a **common dialog box**, and the **Find** result list.*

NOTE: *Depending on how Windows is set, when you open a folder within a folder, its contents may show in the current window or in a new folder window. See **Set Browse Option for Folder Windows**, page 57.*

Open a File or Folder

- Double-click desired .... *file or folder icon*

Open Any File or Folder on Your Computer

— FROM DESKTOP —

1   Double-click ....
My Computer

     NOTE: *If the file or folder is on another computer, you can double-click the Network Neighborhood icon.*

2   Double-click .... *drive icon*
    containing the file or folder to open.

3   Double-click desired .... *file or folder icon*

4   Repeat step **3** as needed.

Open Parent Folder

NOTE: *This option is not available from the desktop or the Find result list.*

1   Show toolbar (page 57).

2   Click **Up One Level** button .... `t..`

Go To a Different Folder

NOTE: *This option is not available from the desktop or the Find result list.*

1   Show toolbar (page 57).

2   Select desired folder in ....

Open Explorer

When Explorer opens, it shows the hierarchy of folders in the **All Folders pane** (left) and the contents of the selected folder in the **Contents pane** (right). See procedures in this section for help on managing files and folders from Explorer.

NOTE: You can run Explorer multiple times and drag items between each Explorer window.

Using Start Button

1 Click . . . . 📇**Start**

2 Point to . . . . 📇 **Programs** ▶

3 Click . . . . 🔍 **Windows Explorer**

By Right-Clicking

1 Right-click desired . . . . **drive or folder icon**

NOTE: You can also right-click permanent folders such as: My Computer, Network Neighborhood and Recycle Bin.

2 Click . . . . **Explore**

By Shift, Double-Clicking

1 Click desired . . . . **drive or folder icon**

NOTE: Step **1** prevents the Shift key in step **2** from creating a multiple selection.

2 Press Shift and double-click the . . . . **drive or folder icon**

Size Explorer All Folders and Contents Panes

1 Point to . . . . **split bar**
Pointer becomes a ↔

2 Drag . . . . **split bar outline**
left or right.

Use Explorer to Browse Folders and Open Files

NOTE: *Explorer shows the hierarchy of folders in the **All Folders pane** (left pane) and the contents of the selected folder in the **Contents pane** (right pane). The current folder name appears in the **Go to a different folder** list box on the toolbar.*

Open Any Folder

- Click . . . . *folder icon*
  in All Folders pane.

  OR

  Double-click . . . . *folder icon*
  in Contents pane.

Go To a Different Folder

1 Show toolbar (page 57).

2 Select desired folder in . . . .

Open Parent Folder

1 Show toolbar (page 57).

2 Click **Up One Level** button . . . . $\boxed{\mathsf{t..}}$

Expand Folder Levels

— *FROM ALL FOLDERS PANE* —

- Click . . . . $\boxed{+}$
  to the left of folder to show folders it contains.

Collapse Folder Levels

— *FROM ALL FOLDERS PANE* —

- Click . . . . $\boxed{-}$
  to the left of folder to hide folders it contains.

Open a File

- Double-click . . . . *file icon*
  in Contents pane.

Use Common Dialog Boxes

*Windows uses common dialog boxes to help you locate, select,
save and open files. In a common dialog box, the **list of items** shows
the contents of the current folder — the folder name in the **Look in** list box.*

— FROM ANY COMMON DIALOG BOX —

*NOTE: You will use the common dialog box when you browse to create a
shortcut or when you select Browse from the Run dialog box.
Page 12 illustrates a common dialog box and its parts.*

Open Any Folder

• Select desired folder in .... **Look in:** [▼]

Open a Folder Appearing in List of Items

• Double-click desired .... ***folder icon***
in list of items.

Open Parent Folder

• Click **Up One Level** button .... [t.·]

Limit File Names Displayed in the List of Items

1 Type filespec in .... **File name:** [   ]

   *NOTE: You must include a wildcard (? or *) to limit files displayed.
   For example, type S* to show only files beginning with S.*

2 Press .... [⏎]

View Specific File Types in List of Items

• Select file type in .... **Files of type:** [▼]

Open File Appearing in List of Items

• Double-click .... ***file icon***

OR

1 Click .... ***file icon***
in list of items.

2 Click .... [Open   ]

Continued ...

Use Common Dialog Boxes (continued)

Create New Folder in Current Folder

*   Click **Create New Folder** button . . . .

Set Appearance of Icons

*   Click **List** button . . . .

    OR

    Click **Details** button . . . .

Common Dialog Box — Right-Click Options

1   Right-click . . . . *file or folder icon*
    A shortcut menu appears.
    NOTE: Items on menu depend upon selection in list.

2   Click appropriate shortcut menu item.
    Shortcut menu items may include: *Copy, Create Shortcut, Cut, Delete,
    Edit, Explore, Find, Open/Open With, Print, Properties, Quick View,
    Rename, Select, Send To, Sharing*

Common Dialog Box — Right-Drag Options

1   Right-drag . . . . *file or folder icon*
    onto destination item.
    A menu appears.

2   Click appropriate menu item.
    Right-drag menu items may include: *Copy Here, Create Shortcut(s)
    Here, Move Here, Open With*

Common Dialog Box — Other File Management Options

For more information, see the following:
Copy Files and Folders, page 66.
Move Files and Folders, page 68.
Rename Files and Folders, page 65.
Delete Files and Folders, page 69.

Set Browse Option for Folder Windows

NOTE: This setting will affect all folder windows.

— FROM MOST FOLDER WINDOWS—

1   Click . . . . **V̲iew, O̲ptions...**

2   Select . . .   ◯ **Browse folders using a s̲eparate window**
                       for each folder.

OR

   Select . . .   ◯ **Browse folders by using a si̲ngle window**
                       that changes as you open each folder.

3   Click . . . . | OK |

Close Current Folder Window and All Parent Windows

NOTE: This command is useful when you are using the default browse
options to use a separate window for each folder (see above).

•   Press **Shift** and double-click
   window's **close** button . . . . **☒**

Show or Hide Toolbar

— FROM ANY FOLDER OR EXPLORER WINDOW —

•   Click . . . . **V̲iew, T̲oolbar**
   to select or deselect.

Show or Hide Status Bar

— FROM ANY FOLDER OR EXPLORER WINDOW —

•   Click . . . . **V̲iew, Status B̲ar**
   to select or deselect.

Set Appearance of Files and Folders

*Sets appearance of files or folders in a **folder window**, the **Explorer
Contents** pane, a **common browse dialog box** (Lists and Details only),
and the **Find** result list.*

Using Menu

NOTE: This method is not available from a common browse dialog box.

1 Click . . . . **View**

2 Select one of the following:

• Click . . . . **Large Icons**

• Click . . . . **Small Icons**

• Click . . . . **List**

• Click . . . . **Details**

Using Toolbar

NOTE: This method is not available from the Find window.

1 Show toolbar (page 57).

2 Click desired button on toolbar:

• **Large Icons** . . . .

• **Small Icons** . . . .

• **List** . . . .

• **Details** . . . .

Arrange Icons

Positions icons on the **desktop**, in a **folder window**, and the **Explorer** Contents pane.

— FROM DESKTOP, FOLDER OR EXPLORER WINDOW —

1   If necessary, set appearance of files and folders to Large or Small Icons (page 58).

2   Select items to arrange (page 64).

3   Drag . . . . **selection outline** to desired position.

   *NOTE: If items do not remain where you placed them,
        deselect the Auto Arrange option (page 61).*

Line Up Icons

Aligns icons evenly (in relation to one another) on the **desktop**, in a **folder window**, the **Explorer** Contents pane, and the **Find** result list.

NOTE: Appearance of icons (page 58) must be set to Large or Small.

By Right-Clicking

1   Right-click empty area on . . . . **desktop**

   or . . . . **folder workspace**

   or . . . . **Explorer Contents pane**

   or . . . . **Find result list**

2   Click . . . . **Line up Icons**

Using Menu

NOTE: This method is not available from the desktop.

1   If necessary, set appearance of files and folders to Large or Small Icons (page 58).

2   Click . . . . **View, Line up Icons**

Arrange Files and Folders in Sort Order

*Arranges files and folders in sort order on the **desktop**, in a **folder window**, the **Explorer** Contents pane, the **Find** result list, and a **common dialog box**. Sort options with depend on the type of folder or workspace.*

By Right-Clicking

1   Right-click empty area on .... *desktop*

     or .... *folder workspace*

     or .... *Explorer Contents pane*

     or .... *Find result list*

     or .... *common dialog box workspace*

2   Point to .... **Arrange Icons** ▶

3   Select desired option:

     Folder or desktop: *by Name, by Type, by Size, by Date*
     My Computer folder: *by Drive Letter, by Type, by Size, by Free Space*
     Network Neighborhood folder: *by Name, by Comment*
     Find result list: *by Name, by Folder, by Type, by Size, by Date*
     Common dialog box: *by Name, by Type, by Size, by Date*

Using Menu

NOTE: *This method is not available from the desktop or a common dialog box.*

1   Click .... **View**

2   Point to .... **Arrange Icons** ▶

3   Select desired option:

     Folder: *by Name, by Type, by Size, by Date*
     My Computer folder: *by Drive Letter, by Type, by Size, by Free Space*
     Network Neighborhood folder: *by Name, by Comment*
     Find result list: *by Name, by Folder, by Type, by Size, by Date*

Continued ...

Arrange Files and Folders in Sort Order (continued)

Using Column Headings

NOTE: This method is not available from the desktop.

1   Set appearance of files and folders to Details (page 58).

2   Click .... *column heading*
   to sort by.

   *NOTE: Click column heading again to switch
   between ascending and descending order.*

Set Auto Arrangement of Icons

*Select to arrange icons automatically when appearance of icons (page 58) is
set to Large or Small.*

By Right-Clicking

1   Right-click empty area on .... *desktop*

   or .... *folder workspace*

   or .... *Explorer Contents pane*

   or .... *Find result list*

2   Point to .... Arrange **I**cons ▶

3   Click .... **A**uto Arrange
   to select or deselect.

Using Menu

*NOTE: This method is not available from the desktop or a
   common dialog box.*

1   Click ....**V**iew

2   Point to .... Arrange **I**cons ▶

3   Click .... **A**uto Arrange
   to select or deselect.

Refresh List of Files and Folders

— FROM ANY FOLDER OR EXPLORER WINDOW —

- Click . . . . <u>V</u>iew, <u>R</u>efresh

  OR

  Press **F5**

Set View Options for Files and Folders

— FROM ANY FOLDER OR EXPLORER WINDOW —

1 Click . . . . <u>V</u>iew, <u>O</u>ptions...

FROM VIEW

2 Select . . . . ◯ <u>S</u>how all files

  OR

  Select . . . . ◯ **Hide files of these <u>t</u>ypes:**

  NOTE: The list box displays files that will be hidden.

3 Select one or more of the following:

  ☐ **Display the full MS-DOS <u>p</u>ath in the title bar**

  ☐ **Hide MS-DOS file <u>e</u>xtensions for files types that are registered**

  ☐ **Include <u>d</u>escription bar for right and left panes**
  NOTE: This setting is for Explorer only.

4 Click . . . . OK

Create Folders

Creates a new folder from the **desktop,** *a* **folder window,** *the* **Explorer Contents** *pane, and a* **common dialog box.**

By Right-Clicking

1 Right-click empty area on . . . . ***desktop***

  or . . . . ***folder workspace***

  or . . . . ***Explorer Contents pane***

  or . . . . ***common dialog box workspace***

2 Point to . . . . **New** ▶

3 Click . . . . **Folder**
  A folder icon appears with the temporary name selected.

4 Type or edit . . . . ***folder name***
  *NOTE: Press left arrow key to edit the folder name,
      or type a new folder name.*

5 Press . . . . ⏎

Using Menu

NOTE: This method is not available from the desktop.

1 Click . . . . **File**

2 Point to . . . . **New** ▶

3 Click . . . . **Folder**
  A folder icon appears with the temporary name selected.

4 Type or edit . . . . ***folder name***
  *NOTE: Press left arrow key to edit the folder name,
      or type a new folder name.*

5 Press . . . . ⏎

Select Files and Folders

*Selects files and folders from the **desktop**, a **folder** window, the **Explorer** Contents pane, and the **Find** result list.*

Select One File or Folder

* Click . . . . *file or folder icon*

Select Multiple Files and Folders

* Press **Ctrl** and click desired . . . . *files and folders*

Select a Group of Files and Folders

1 Point to . . . . *blank area*
  near items to select.

2 Drag . . . . *an outline*
  over desired . . . . *files and folders*

Select All Files and Folders

NOTE: This option is not available from the desktop.

* Click . . . . **Edit, Select All**

  OR

  Press . . . . **Ctrl** + **A**

Select Most, But Not All, Files and Folders

NOTE: This method is not available from the desktop.

1 Press **Ctrl** and click . . . . *files and folders*
  you do not want to select.

2 Click . . . . **Edit, Invert Selection**

Deselect Files and Folders

* Click . . . . *any blank area*

Rename Files and Folders

*Renames files or folders from the **desktop**, a **folder window**, the **Explorer** Contents pane, a **common browse dialog box**, and the **Find** result list. File names may contain spaces and can be as long as 255 characters. They cannot, however, contain the following characters:* \ * ? " < > |

By Clicking

1 Click desired . . . . *file or folder icon*

2 Click . . . . *icon name*
Cursor appears at end of name.

3 Type or edit name . . . . *name*
NOTE: Press left arrow key to edit the name, or type a new name.

4 Press . . . .

By Right-Clicking

1 Right-click desired . . . . *file or folder icon*

2 Click . . . . **Rename**
Windows highlights the current name, and a cursor appears at the end of the name.

3 Type or edit name . . . . *name*
NOTE: Press left arrow key to edit the name, or type a new name.

4 Press . . . .

Using Menu

NOTE: This method is not available from the desktop.

1 Click desired . . . . *file or folder icon*

2 Click . . . . **File, Rename**
Windows highlights the current name and a cursor appears at the end of the name.

3 Type or edit name . . . . *name*
NOTE: Press left arrow key to edit the name, or type a new name.

4 Press . . . .

Set File and Folder Attributes

Sets attributes of files or folders from the **desktop**, *a* **folder window**,
the **Explorer** *Contents pane, a* **common browse dialog box**, *and the* **Find**
result list.

CAUTION: You should not change the attributes of a file or folder
unless you completely understand the effect of the change.

1   Right-click desired . . . . *file or folder icon*

2   Click . . . . **P**r**operties...**

3   Select or deselect attribute options:

   •   Click . . . . ☐ **R**e**ad Only**

   •   Click . . . . ☐ **Ar**c**hive**

   •   Click . . . . ☐ **Hi**d**den**

   •   Click . . . . ☐ **S**y**stem**

4   Click . . . . | OK |

Copy Files and Folders

Copies files and folders from the **desktop**, *a* **folder window**, *the* **Explorer**
Contents pane, a **common browse dialog box**, *and the* **Find** *result list.*

By Dragging

1   Arrange desktop so that items to copy and destination folder
are in view.
NOTE: The destination folder can be a window, icon or the desktop.

2   Select files and folders to copy (page 64).

3   Press **Ctrl** and drag . . . . *selection*
over destination folder window, folder icon or desktop.
A plus sign appears, and Windows highlights the destination icon
or shows selection outline over destination.
NOTE: You do not have to press **Ctrl** *when copying items*
to a folder on another drive.

4   Release mouse button (and key, if used) to complete copy.

Continued ...

Copy Files and Folders (continued)

Using Menu

NOTE: This method is not available from the desktop.

1 Open folder (page 52) containing items to copy.

2 Select files and folders (page 64) to copy.

3 Click . . . . **Edit, Copy**

To paste copy on desktop:

a Right-click empty area on . . . . *desktop*

b Click . . . . **Paste**

To paste copy in another folder:

a Open (page 52) destination folder.

b Click . . . . **Edit, Paste**

Using Send To Command

Copies selected items to the shortcuts in the Send To folder. By default, Windows adds a shortcut to drive A: to this folder.

NOTE: If you add shortcuts to the Windows\SendTo folder, they will also appear on the Send To menu.

1 Select files and folders to copy (page 64).

2 Right-click . . . . *selection*

3 Point to . . . . **Send To** ▶

4 Click . . . . *destination item*
on Send To menu.

Undo Your Last Action

Reverses your last action, such as your last move, copy, rename and delete.

1 Right-click empty area on . . . ***desktop or folder workspace***

2 Click . . . . **Undo** . . .
NOTE: The Undo menu option includes the name of your last action.

Move Files and Folders

*Moves files and folders from the **desktop**, a **folder window**, the **Explorer** Contents pane, a **common browse dialog box**, and the **Find** result list.*

By Dragging

1 Arrange desktop so that items to move and destination folder are in view.
NOTE: The destination folder can be a window, icon or the desktop.

2 Select files and folders to move (page 64).

3 Drag . . . . *selection* over destination folder.
Windows highlights destination icon or shows selection outline over destination window.

If destination is a folder on another drive:

• Press and hold . . . . **Shift**

4 Release mouse button (and key, if used) to complete move.

Using Menu

NOTE: This method is not available from the desktop.

1 Open folder (page 52) containing items to move.

2 Select files and folders (page 64) to move.

3 Click . . . . **Edit, Cut**
The cut file appears ghosted.

To paste on desktop:

a Right-click empty area on . . . . *desktop*

b Click . . . . **Paste**

To paste in another folder or drive:

a Open (page 52) destination folder or drive.

b Click . . . . **Edit, Paste**

Delete Files and Folders

Deletes files and folders from the **desktop,** *a* **folder window,** *the* **Explorer**
Contents pane, a **common browse dialog box,** *and the* **Find** *result list.*
NOTE: Unless you configure Windows differently, deleted files are stored in
the Recycle Bin until you purge them, or until deleted items take up
a specified percentage of available hard disk space.

By Dragging

1   Select files and folders (page 64) to delete.

2   Drag . . . . *selection*

over . . . .

Recycle Bin

Windows highlights the Recycle Bin.
NOTE: To permanently delete the selection
(bypass the Recycle Bin), press **Shift** *while dragging selection.*

3   Release mouse button when Recycle Bin is highlighted.

By Right-Clicking

1   Select files and folders (page 64) to delete.

2   Right-click . . . . *selection*

3   Click . . . . **Delete**
NOTE: To permanently delete the selection
(bypass the Recycle Bin), press **Shift + Del.**

4   Click . . . . | Yes |
to confirm deletion.

Using Menu

NOTE: This method is not available from the desktop.

1   Select files and folders (page 64) to delete.

2   Click . . . . **File, Delete**
NOTE: To permanently delete the selection
(bypass the Recycle Bin), press **Shift** *while clicking* Delete.

3   Click . . . . | Yes |
to confirm deletion.

Restore Items in Recycle Bin to Original Folders

— FROM DESKTOP —

- Double-click . . . .   Recycle Bin

  ### To restore last deleted item:

  - Click . . . . **Edit, Undo Delete**

  ### To restore specific items:

  a Select files and folders (page 64) to restore.

  b Click . . . . **File, Restore**

Purge Items in Recycle Bin

CAUTION: *Items that are purged (deleted) from the Recycle Bin cannot be restored.*

— FROM DESKTOP —

- Double-click . . . .   Recycle Bin

  ### To purge all items:

  a Click . . . . **File, Empty Recycle Bin**

  b Click . . . . | Yes |

  ### To purge specific items:

  a Select files and folders (page 64) to purge.

  b Click . . . . **File, Delete**

  c Click . . . . | Yes |

NOTE: *You can quickly purge all items in the Recycle Bin by right-clicking the Recycle Bin icon and selecting Empty Recycle Bin. This method does not allow you review the items you are purging; therefore, you should use this method with caution.*

Set Recycle Bin Properties

— FROM DESKTOP —

1 Right-click . . . . Recycle Bin

2 Click . . . . **P̲roperties...**

To set independent or global drive configuration:

- Select . . . . ◯ **C̲onfigure drives independently**

  OR

  Select . . . . ◯ **U̲se one setting for all drives**

To set immediate deletion of files:

— FROM GLOBAL OR SPECIFIC DRIVE TAB —

- Select . . . . . . ☐ **Do not move files to the R̲ecycle Bin. Remove files immediately on delete**

  WARNING: *If you select this option, you cannot recover deleted files.*

To set maximum size of Recycle Bin:

— FROM GLOBAL OR SPECIFIC DRIVE TAB —

- Drag slider . . . .
  left or right to set percent of each drive.

To remove delete confirmation dialog box:

- Deselect . . . . ☑ **D̲isplay delete confirmation dialog**

3 Click . . . . | OK |

Format Disks

— FROM DESKTOP —

1 Double-click . . . . My Computer

2 Right-click . . . . ***drive icon***
containing diskette to format.

3 Click . . . . **For̲mat...**

4 Select disk capacity in . . . . **Capacity:** [▼]

5 Select one format type:

- Click . . . . ◯ **Q̲uick (erase)**
  to reformat disk quickly without checking for disk errors.

- Click . . . . ◯ **F̲ull**
  to format or reformat disk and check for disk errors.

- Click . . . . ◯ **Copy system files o̲nly**
  to transfer system files to a formatted disk.

To label disk when formatting:

- Type desired label in . . . . **L̲abel:** [   ]

To remove label when formatting:

- Select . . . . ☐ **N̲o label**

To report results of formatting when done:

- Select . . . . ☐ **D̲isplay summary when finished**

To make disk bootable after formatting:

- Select . . . . ☐ **Copy sy̲stem files**

6 Click . . . . [S̲tart]

Copy Floppy Disks

— FROM DESKTOP —

1 Double-click . . . . My Computer

2 Right-click . . . . ***drive icon***
containing diskette to copy.

3 Click . . . . **Copy Disk...**

4 Select source in . . . . **Copy from:** list box

5 Select destination in . . . . **Copy to:** list box

6 Insert disk(s) in disk drive.

7 Click . . . . | Start |

8 Follow screen prompts.

9 Click . . . . | Close |

View and Set Disk Properties

— FROM DESKTOP —

1 Double-click . . . . My Computer

2 Right-click desired . . . . ***drive icon***

3 Click . . . . **Properties**

FROM GENERAL

View drive information:
Windows shows the following drive information:
- *Label, Type, Used space, Free space, Capacity*
- *a chart showing percentage of used and free space on the disk.*

To add or edit drive label:
- Type or edit label in . . . . **Label:** | |

4 Click . . . . | OK |

Use Disk Tools

Reports the last time you used ScanDisk, Backup and Disk Defragmenter on a specific disk and provides commands to use those disk tools.

— FROM DESKTOP —

1 Double-click . . . . My Computer

2 Right-click desired . . . . **drive icon**

3 Click . . . . **Properties**

> FROM *TOOLS*

View status of disk tools usage for this drive

Windows shows the following information:
- *Error-checking status*
- *Backup status*
- *Defragmentation status*

To check drive for errors:

a Click . . . . Check Now...

b Select desired Scandisk options (page 250).

To backup files on drive:

a Click . . . . Backup Now...

b Select desired Backup options (page 219–221).

To defragment drive:

a Click . . . . Defragment Now...

b Select desired Disk Defragmenter options (page 208).

4 Click . . . . OK

Create a Data File

*Creates a data file on the **desktop**, in a **folder window**, in Explorer Contents pane, and a **common dialog box**. The file created is of a type associated with an application Windows recognizes as having been installed.*

By Right-Clicking

1 Right-click empty area on . . . . **desktop**

or . . . . **folder workspace**

or . . . . **Explorer Contents pane**

or . . . . **common dialog box workspace**

2 Point to . . . . **Ne̲w** ▶

3 Click . . . . **desired file type**
on bottom of submenu.
NOTE: File types for registered applications automatically appear on this menu.

A file icon appears with a temporary file name selected.

4 Type or edit file name . . . . **file name**
NOTE: Press left arrow key to edit the file name, or type new file name. To retain the association with the application, do not change the file name extension.

5 Press . . . .

Using Menu

NOTE: This method is not available from the desktop.

1 Click . . . . **F̲ile**

2 Point to . . . . **Ne̲w** ▶

3 Click . . . . **desired file type**
on bottom of submenu.
NOTE: File types for registered applications automatically appear on this menu.

A file icon appears with a temporary file name selected.

4 Type or edit file name . . . . **file name**
NOTE: Press left arrow key to edit the file name, or type a new file name. To retain the association with the application, do not change the file name extension.

5 Press . . . .

Open an Application or Data File

Opens applications or associated data files.

Using Start — Programs Menu

1   Click . . . .   📁 Start

2   Click . . . . *item to open*
    at top of Start menu.

OR

   a   Point to . . . .   📁 <u>P</u>rograms ▶

   b   Click . . . . *item to open*

     OR

     1.   Point to . . . . 📁 *subfolder name* ▶
        containing item to open.
        NOTE: Repeat this step as needed.

     2.   Click . . . . *item to open*

Using Start — Documents Menu

Opens recently used documents.

1   Click . . . .   📁 Start

2   Point to . . . .   📂 <u>D</u>ocuments ▶

3   Click . . . . *document name*
    Windows opens the file using the application it is associated with.

By Right-Clicking

— FROM DESKTOP, FOLDER, FIND OR EXPLORER WINDOW —

1   Right-click . . . . *application or data file icon*

2   Click . . . . <u>O</u>pen

OR

   a   Click . . . . **Open <u>W</u>ith...**

   b   Select application to open file with in . . . . **list box**

   c   Click . . . . | OK |

Continued ...

Open Application or Data File (continued)

Using Start — Run Command

1 Click . . . . 🎐 Start

2 Click . . . . 📰 **Run...**

3 **a** Type or select path and file name in . . **Open** [_____ ▼]

     NOTE: Windows stores a command history in the Open list box.

   b Click . . . . [_____OK_____]

   OR

   a Click . . . . [_Browse..._]

   b Use the common dialog box (page 55) to open the file.

4 Click . . . . [_____OK_____]

Using MS-DOS Command Prompt

1 Type program name . . . . *program name*

   NOTE: You can also run Windows applications from
           the MS-DOS prompt.

2 Press . . . . ⏎

By Dragging

— FROM DESKTOP, FOLDER, FIND OR EXPLORER WINDOW —

- Drag . . . . *associated data file icon*
  onto desired . . . . . *application or application shortcut icon*

By Double-Clicking

— FROM DESKTOP, FOLDER, FIND OR EXPLORER WINDOW —

- Double-click . . . . . *application, data file, or shortcut icon*
  to open.

  NOTE: If the data file is not associated with an application, the Open
        *With dialog box appears. See **Change Application that Starts***
        ***when Opening a Data File**, page 82.*

Start an MS-DOS Session

Using Start — Programs Menu

1   Click .... **Start**

2   Point to .... **Programs** ►

3   Click .... **MS-DOS Prompt**

Using Start — Run Command

1   Click .... **Start**

2   Click .... **Run...**

3   Type COMMAND.COM in .... **Open** [▼]

4   Click .... **OK**

Display Help for an MS-DOS Command

— FROM MS-DOS WINDOW OR SCREEN —

1   Type command name .... *command name*

2   Type .... **/ ?**

To display one screen of help text at a time:

•   Type .... **| M O R E**

3   Press .... **↵**

    EXAMPLE: DIR /? |MORE

MS-DOS Commmand List

NOTE: *Also see **Display Help for an MS-DOS Command** on the previous page.*

- You can use the following commands from the MS-DOS prompt:

  ATTRIB, BREAK, CD, CHCP, CHDIR, CHKDSK, CLS, COMMAND, COPY, CTTY, DATE, DRVSPACE, DEBUG, DEFRAG, DEL (ERASE), DELTREE, DIR, DISKCOPY, DOSKEY, EDIT, EMM386, ERASE, EXIT, EXPAND, FC, FDISK, FIND, FOR, FORMAT, KEYB, LABEL, LOADFIX, LOADHIGH (LH), MD, MEM, MKDIR, MODE, MORE, MOVE, MSD, NET, NLSFUNC, PATH, PROMPT, RD, REN, RENAME, RMDIR, SCANDISK, SET, SETVER, SMARTDRV, SORT, START, SUBST, SYS, TIME, TYPE, VER, VERIFY, VOL, XCOPY

Run MS-DOS Session Full-Screen or in a Window

— FROM MS-DOS WINDOW OR SCREEN —

- Press .... `Alt` + `⏎`
  to toggle between running application full screen and in a window.

Close an MS-DOS Session

— FROM MS-DOS WINDOW OR SCREEN —

- If necessary, exit MS-DOS application running in MS-DOS session.

  ### To close MS-DOS session running in a window:

  - Click **close** button .... `✕`
    on right side of window's title bar.

  ### To close MS-DOS session running full screen:

  a Type .... `E` `X` `I` `T`

  b Press .... `⏎`

Close a Windows Application

NOTE: If you have not saved the data you are working with, the application will prompt you to save it.

Using Close Button

- Click close button . . . . ☒
  on right side of window's title bar.

Using Keyboard

- Press . . . . Alt + F4

Using Control Symbol

1 Click . . . . *control symbol*
  on left side of window's title bar.

2 Click . . . . **Close**

Using Taskbar

1 Right-click . . . . *application button*
  on taskbar.

2 Click . . . . **Close**

Set Application or Data File to Open on Startup

1 Click . . . . | 🏴 Start |

2 Point to . . . . 🦗 **Settings** ▸

3 Click . . . . 🖳 **Taskbar...**

_____| *FROM START MENU PROGRAMS* |_____

4 Click . . . . | Add... |

5 Click . . . . | Browse... |

6 Use the common dialog box (page 55) to open the file.
After opening the desired file, its path and filename appear in the Command line text box.

7 Click . . . . | Next > |

8 Click . . . . 🗂 **StartUp**
in list to select it.
NOTE: You may have to scroll down to the StartUp folder which is contained in the Programs folder.

9 Click . . . . | Next > |

10 If desired, edit name for shortcut in . . . . | |

11 Click . . . . | Finish |

12 Click . . . . | OK |

NOTES: You'll have to restart your computer for this change to take effect.
*See **Remove Items from the Start or Programs Menu**, page 87, for information about removing applications and data files that open on startup.*

Change Application that Starts when Opening a Data File

Changes the application that starts when you want to open data files of a certain type (files having a specific filename extension).

— FROM ANY FOLDER OR EXPLORER WINDOW —

1 Click .... **Vi̲ew, O̲ptions...**

FROM *FILE TYPES*

2 Select file type to change in ... **Registered file t̲ypes: list box**
Windows displays extension for file and application that opens it in File type details section.

3 Click .... | Edit... |

4 Select *open command* in .... **A̲ctions: list box**

5 Click .... | Edit... |

6 Type path and file
name in ... **Appli̲cation used to perform action:** | |

OR

a Click .... | Browse... |

b Use the common dialog box (page 55) to open (select)
the application file.

c Click .... | OK |

7 Select or deselect .... ☐ **Enable Q̲uick View**

8 Select or deselect .... ☐ **Alw̲ays show extension**

9 Click .... | Close |
to close Edit File Type dialog box.

10 Click .... | Close |
to close Options dialog box.

Associate a New File Type with an Application

Sets the application that starts when you want to open data files of a certain type (files having a specific file name extension).

— FROM ANY FOLDER OR EXPLORER WINDOW —

1 Click . . . . **View, Options...**

FROM **FILE TYPES**

2 Click . . . . | New Type... |

3 Type description for file
type in . . . . **Description of type:** [ ]

4 Type three character file name
extension for file type in . . **Associated extension:** [ ]

> *NOTE: MIME (Multipurpose Internet Mail Extensions) options may
> appear if you have installed Internet Explorer.*

5 Click . . . . | New... |

6 Type name of action in . . . . **Action:** [ ]

> *EXAMPLE: &Open with Notepad (& specifies O as accelerator key)*

7 Type path and application file
name in . . . **Application used to perform action:** [ ]

OR

Click . . . . | Browse... |

then use the common dialog box (page 55)
to open (select) the application file.

> *NOTE: Select **Use DDE** if the application or file type supports
> Dynamic Data Exchange commands. Then, Windows will
> prompt you for additional DDE information. With DDE, you
> can also set other actions (such as print).*

8 Click . . . . | OK |

9 Select or deselect . . . . ☐ **Enable Quick View**

10 Select or deselect . . . . ☐ **Always show extension**

11 Click . . . . | Close |

to close Add New File Type dialog box.

12 Click . . . . | Close |

Add One Item to the Start or Programs Menu

Adds a menu item (shortcut) to the top of the Start menu, the Programs menu or to a Programs submenu.

Using Start — Settings Menu

1 Click . . . . 🏁 **Start**

2 Point to . . . . 🗒 **Settings ▶**

3 Click . . . . 🏁 **Taskbar...**

FROM START MENU PROGRAMS

4 Click . . . . Add...

5 Type path and file name
for menu item in . . . . **Command line:** ▭

OR

  a Click . . . . Browse...

  b Use the common dialog box (page 55) to open the file.
The path and file name appear in Command line text box.

6 Click . . . . Next >

7 **a** Click . . . . *folder icon*
     in which you want item to appear.

  b Click . . . . Next >

  OR

To create new folder for item:

  a Click . . . . *folder icon*
     in which new folder will be created.

  b Click . . . . New Folder...

  c Type . . . . *new folder name*

  d Press . . . . ⏎

Continued ...

Add One Item to the Start or Programs Menu (continued)

8 If desired, edit name for shortcut to appear on menu in . . . . **Select a name for the shortcut:** [ ]

9 Click . . . . Finish

10 Click . . . . OK

By Dragging

Adds a menu item (shortcut) to the top of the Start menu.

1 Find (page 47) or open folder (page 52) containing item to add to top of Start menu.

2 Drag . . . . ***item icon***
onto . . . . Start

Clear Items on Documents Menu

Clears all shortcuts to recently opened documents on Documents menu.

1 Click . . . . Start

2 Point to . . . . **Settings ▸**

3 Click . . . . **Taskbar...**

FROM ***START MENU PROGRAMS***

4 Click . . . . Clear
in Documents menu section.

5 Click . . . . OK

Add Multiple Items to the Start or Programs Menu

Adds shortcuts and folders to the Start Menu folder or subfolder, such as the Programs folder. These items then appear on the Start menu or one of its submenus when you click the Start button on the taskbar.

1 Right-click . . . . `⊞Start`

2 Click . . . . **Open**
    Windows opens the Start Menu folder.

To add items (shortcuts) to the Start menu:

a If necessary, open Start Menu subfolder to receive shortcut.

b Open folder containing item to add to menu.

c Right-drag desired . . . . *item*
    onto destination . . . . . . *Start Menu folder or subfolder*

d Click . . . . **Create Shortcut(s) Here**

e Repeat steps **b-d** for each item to add to menu.

To add a folder to the Start menu:

a If desired, double-click folder (such as the Programs folder) to receive new folder.
    *NOTE: Folders you add to the Start Menu folder (without doing step **a**), will appear at the top of the Start menu.*

b Right-click . . . . *folder workspace*

c Point to . . . . **New** ▶

d Click . . . . **Folder**
    A folder icon appears with the temporary name selected.

e Type or edit . . . . *folder name*
    NOTE: Press left arrow key to edit the folder name, or type a new folder name. The name you type will appear as a submenu in the selected menu folder.

f Press . . . . `⏎`

3 Click Start Menu window's **close** button . . . . `✕`
    to close it.

Remove Items from the Start or Programs Menu

Removes Start menu items (folders and shortcuts) from the top of the Start menu or one of its subfolders, such as the Programs folder.

1 Click . . . . **🏁 Start**

2 Point to . . . . **🎛 Settings ▶**

3 Click . . . . **🗔 Taskbar...**

_____ FROM *START MENU PROGRAMS* _____

4 Click . . . . **Remove...**
in Customize Start Menu section.

> *NOTE:* For steps 5 and 6, you may have to use the scroll arrows to bring the desired folder or shortcut into view.

5 If necessary, double-click . . . . ***folder icon***
containing item to remove.

6 Click . . . . ***file or folder icon***
to remove.

> *NOTE:* If you select a folder, you will remove all the shortcuts and other folders it may contain.

7 Click . . . . **Remove**

8 Repeat steps **5–7** for each item to remove.

9 Click . . . . **Close**

10 Click . . . . **OK**

Create a Shortcut

*Creates shortcuts on the **desktop**, in a **folder window**, in Explorer Contents pane, or a **common dialog box**. **Shortcuts** are files containing pointers to other items, such as folders, data files and applications that you open frequently.*

This procedure shows two ways to create a shortcut:

- **From destination folder:** *You want to create shortcuts in the current folder to items in other folders.*

- **From source folder:** *You are in a folder containing an item to which you want to create a shortcut. You want to place the shortcut on the desktop or in another folder.*

   When you create a shortcut, an icon with a jump arrow (see page 7) appears.

From Destination Folder

1 Right-click empty area on . . . . *desktop*

   or . . . . *folder workspace*

   or . . . . *Explorer Contents pane*

   or . . . . *common dialog box workspace*

2 Point to . . . . **New** ▶

3 Click . . . . **Shortcut**

4 Type path and file name of item
   to create shortcut to in . . . . **Command line:** [   ]

   OR

   a Click . . . . [Browse...]

   b Use the common dialog box (page 55) to open the file.

5 Click . . . . [Next >]

6 Type or edit shortcut name in . . . . [   ]

7 Click . . . . [Finish]

Continued ...

Create Shortcut (continued)

From Source Folder

By Right-Clicking

1 Right-click . . . . *item*
  to create shortcut to.

2 Click . . . . **Copy**

3 Open . . . . *destination folder*

  NOTE: Destination folder can be a window or the desktop.

4 Right-click empty area in . . . . *desktop or folder workspace*

5 Click . . . . **Paste Shortcut**

By Right-Dragging

1 Arrange desktop so item to create shortcut to and destination
  folder are in view.

  NOTE: Destination folder can be a window, icon or the desktop.

2 Right-drag . . . . *item*
  to create shortcut to onto . . . . *destination folder*

3 Click . . . . **Create Shortcut(s) Here**

Using Menu

1 Arrange desktop so item to create shortcut to and destination
  folder are in view.

  NOTE: Destination folder can be a window, icon or the desktop.

2 Click . . . . *item*
  to create a shortcut to.

3 Click . . . . **File, Create Shortcut**

  Windows creates the shortcut in the source folder.

4 Drag . . . . *shortcut icon*
  onto . . . . *destination folder*

  NOTE: Destination folder can be a window, icon or the desktop.

Set Properties of a Shortcut

*Changes properties of a shortcut on the **desktop**, in a **folder window**, in **Explorer** Contents pane, and a **common dialog box**.*

1 Right-click desired . . . . ***shortcut icon***

2 Click . . . . **P̲roperties**

> FROM SHORTCUT

To change name and location of item to which shortcut points:

- Type path and file name in . . . . **T̲arget:** [ ]

To set working directory for shortcut item:

- Type path to folder in . . . . **S̲tart in:** [ ]

  NOTE: Windows provides the path typed here to applications that need to know the location or related files.

To set shortcut key to run or switch to application:

- Press combination key in . . . . . **Shortcut k̲ey:** [ ]

  *NOTE: Shortcut key must combine **Ctrl** and/or **Alt**, such as **Ctrl + Alt + P**.*

To select initial window state:

- Select desired option in . . . . **R̲un:** [▼]

  Window states include: *Normal window, Minimized and Maximized.*

To open folder containing original target item:

- Click . . . . [F̲ind Target...]

To change shortcut icon:

a Click . . . . [C̲hange Icon...]

b Select desired icon in . . . . **C̲urrent Icon:** list box

c Click . . . . [OK]

3 Click . . . . [OK]

Add or Remove Windows Components

1 Click .... 🏁 **Start**

2 Point to .... 📁 **Settings** ▶

3 Click .... 🖥 **Control Panel**

4 Double-click .... Add/Remove Programs

---

FROM WINDOWS SETUP

To add entire component:

- Click check box next to
  component to add in .... **Components:** list box
  until a dark check mark appears.

To remove entire component:

- Click check box next to
  component to remove in .... **Components:** list box
  until check mark is cleared.

To add/remove parts of component:

a Click name of component in ...... **Components:** list box

b Click .... Details...

c Click check box next to
  component to add/remove in ...... **Components:** list box
  to select or deselect it.

d Repeat step **c** for each item to add or remove.

e Click .... OK

  A shaded check box appears next to component name.

5 Click .... OK

6 If prompted, insert disks or CD and follow instructions.

Install Applications

Installs Windows and DOS applications on your hard disk.

1 Click . . . . `🔳 Start`

2 Point to . . . . `🔧 Settings ▶`

3 Click . . . . `📁 Control Panel`

4 Double-click . . . . `📑 Add/Remove Programs`

FROM INSTALL/UNINSTALL

5 Click . . . . `Install...`

6 Insert setup disk in . . . . ***floppy or CD-ROM drive***

7 Click . . . . `Next >`

> *NOTE: Windows inserts setup command in text box, if found.*
> *You can click Browse and use the common dialog*
> *box (page 55) to locate setup command manually.*

8 Click . . . . `Finish`

9 Follow setup prompts for application.
Windows adds a folder in the Start, Programs menu
(if you added a Windows application) and opens the folder.

Uninstall Applications

Removes Windows applications from your hard disk.

1 Click . . . . `Start`

2 Point to . . . . **Settings** ▶

3 Click . . . . **Control Panel**

4 Double-click . . . . Add/Remove Programs

FROM INSTALL/UNINSTALL

5 Select application to remove in . . . . list box

> NOTE: *This list contains only newer applications Windows can remove automatically.*

6 Click . . . . `Add/Remove...`

Select Open Application or Folder

• Click any part of . . . . *window*
   to select.

   OR

   Click . . . . *application or folder button*
   on taskbar.

   OR

   a Press and hold . . . . `Alt`
      while pressing and releasing . . . . `Tab`
      until desired item is outlined.

   b Release . . . . *keys*
      to select outlined item.

Open a Data File from a Windows Application

1 Click . . . . **File, Open...**

2 Use the common dialog box (page 55) to locate
and open the file.

   *NOTE: Only applications created specifically for Windows 95 will
            use the common dialog box. The common dialog box will
            have a Look in list box from which all drives, including
            network drives, can be selected.*

OR

Select file to open in dialog box.

   NOTE: Refer to the documentation for your application.

Save and Name Data Files from a Windows Application

Copies data in an open application to a new file, or renames an existing file.

1 Click . . . . **File, Save As...**

2 Use the common dialog box (page 55) to open
the destination folder and save the file.

   *NOTE: Only applications created specifically for Windows 95 will
            use the common dialog box. The common dialog box will
            have a Look in list box from which all drives, including
            network drives can be selected.*

OR

Open destination directory and save the file.

   NOTE: Refer to the documentation for your application.

Use Quick View to Preview a Data File

Previews contents of files selected on the **desktop,** *in a* **folder window,** *in* **Explorer** *Contents pane, or a* **common dialog box.**

NOTE: *If the Quick View option is not available, the data file type may not be supported or Quick View may not have been installed.*

By Right-Clicking

1   Right-click . . . . *data file icon*

2   Click . . . . **Q**uick View

Using Menu

NOTE: *This method is not available from the desktop.*

1   Click . . . . *data file icon*

2   Click . . . . **F**ile, **Q**uick View...

By Dragging

1   After viewing first file *(see above).*

2   Drag desired . . . . *data file icon*
     to preview onto . . . . *Quick View window*

Set Quick View to Show Next File in Same Window

1   After viewing first file *(see above).*

2   Click . . . . **V**iew, Replace **W**indow

3   Use the right-click or menu method (above) to view next data file in same Quick View window.

Continued ...

Use Quick View to Preview a Data File (continued)

Toolbar Options for Quick View Window

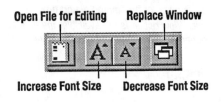

Open File for Editing   **Replace Window**

Increase Font Size   **Decrease Font Size**

Menu Options for Quick View Window

File	
Open File for Editing	Opens file you are previewing for editing.
Exit	Closes Quick View window.

View	
Toolbar	Shows or hides toolbar.
Status Bar	Shows or hides status bar.
Page View	Switches preview mode between document and page view. *NOTE: Page view provides tabs on page corner for viewing other pages.*
Replace Window	Sets Quick View to display subsequent file selections in the same Quick View window when this option is selected.
Landscape	Switches page view between portrait and landscape.
Rotate	Rotates graphic documents when Page View is deselected.
Font...	Sets font for previewing text documents.

Close a Failed Application or Windows Session

Closes an application component or the Windows session when either is not working properly.

- Press . . . . **Ctrl** + **Alt** + **Del**

  The Close Program dialog box appears.

  ## To close a specific application:

  a Click application to close in . . . . *list box*

  NOTE: *Windows adds* (not responding) *next to the name of the failed application or process.*

  b Click . . . . `End Task`

  ## To shut down your computer:

- Click . . . . `Shut Down`

  ## To restart your computer:

  NOTE: *When Windows is not responding properly, you should first try to restart your computer by selecting Shut Down (see above).*

- Press . . . . **Ctrl** + **Alt** + **Del**

Set MS-DOS Application Properties

1   Right-click . . . .   ***DOS application or shortcut icon***
   OR

   — FROM RUNNING MS-DOS APPLICATION —

   a   If running application full-screen,
      run it in a window . . . . **Alt**+**↵**

   b   Right-click . . . . **DOS application title bar**

2   Click . . . . **Properties**

3   Select options or view items described in the tables that follow.
   Tab categories (property sheets) for MS-DOS applications include
   General, Program, Font, Memory, Screen, and Misc.

General	
General information	General information includes: • Type • Location • Size • MS-DOS name • Created • Modified • Accessed

Attributes
   Read-only
   Archive
   Hidden
   System
	Select to set the attributes.
	 *NOTE: Do not change an attribute
	        unless you completely
	        understand the effect of
	        the change.*

NOTE: *General properties are not available for the MS-DOS Prompt.*

Continued ...

Set MS-DOS Application Properties (continued)

Program	
Cmd line	Type path and program name that runs the program.
Working	Type path to folder to set as working directory.
Batch file	Type batch file name to run on startup.
Shortcut key	Press shortcut key (such as Ctrl+Shift+C) to let you quickly run or switch to the program.
Run	Select window state (Normal Window / Minimized / Maximized) to use when application runs.
Close on exit	Select to close the MS-DOS window when you exit the application.

Advanced...	Click to set how to run DOS applications:
	
	Advanced options include:
	• Prevent MS DOS-based programs from detecting Windows
	• Suggest MS-DOS mode* as necessary
	• MS-DOS mode
	  • Warn before entering MS-DOS mode
	  • Use current MS-DOS configuration
	  • Specify a new MS-DOS configuration
	  • CONFIG.SYS for MS-DOS mode
	    AUTOEXEC.BAT for MS-DOS mode
	  • Configuration

Change Icon...	Click to select a new icon for the application.

*MS-DOS mode — sets application to use all of your system resources. When you select this mode, your computer will restart and run only the application. When you quit the application, Windows will restart automatically. This option is useful for applications such as games that cannot run otherwise.

Continued ...

Set MS-DOS Application Properties (continued)

Font	
Available types	
Bitmap only	Select to use this font type when running application in a window.
TrueType only	Select to use this font type when running application in a window.
Both font types	Select to use Bitmap and TrueType fonts when running application in a window.
Font size	Select a font type and size for application when running application in a window. The font size changes the window size.
Window preview	Shows sample window size for selected font.
Font preview	Shows sample of selected font.

Continued ...

Set MS-DOS Application Properties (continued)

Memory	
Conventional memory	
Total	Select amount of required conventional memory (in kilobytes) or select Auto.
Initial environment	Select memory (in bytes) to reserve for MS-DOS COMMAND.COM. If set to Auto, environment is set by SHELL= command in CONFIG.SYS.
Protected	Select to protect system memory from inappropriate use by the application. (Slows performance, but protects system from failures by the program.)
Expanded (EMS) memory	
Total:	Select maximum amount of expanded memory (in kilobytes) the program can use.
	NOTE: If Total is not available, click Details to read an explanation.
Details	Click to show how to enable Total Expanded Memory setting above.
Extended (XMS) memory	
Total:	Select maximum amount of extended memory (in kilobytes) the program can use.
Uses HMA	Select to enable use of high memory area (HMA) for this application.
MS-DOS protected-mode (DPMI) memory	
Total:	Select maximum amount of this memory type (in kilobytes) the program can use.

Continued ...

Set MS-DOS Application Properties (continued)

Screen	
Usage	
Full-screen	Select to run application full-screen.
Window	Select to run application in a window.
Initial si**z**e	Select initial number of lines on the screen for the application.
Window	
Display **t**oolbar	Select to show toolbar when running the application in a window.
Restore settings on startup	Select to restore window settings (such as font and size) when you restart the application.
Performance	
Fast ROM **e**mulation	Deselect if the application uses video functions that are causing problems. Select to improve video performance.
Dynamic **m**emory allocation	Select to allocate memory to other programs as needed.

Continued ...

Set MS-DOS Application Properties (continued)

Misc	
Foreground **Allow scr̲een saver**	Select to enable Windows screen saver when the application is active.
Mouse **Q̲uickEdit**	Select to let you use mouse to select text in application for cut and copy procedures.
Ex̲clusive mode	Select to use mouse in this application only. *NOTE: You will have to press Alt+Space, then select Properties to be able to turn this setting off.*
Background **Always s̲uspend**	Select to suspend use of CPU for this application when another application is active.
Termination **W̲arn if still active**	Select to warn you when you attempt to close the application window when application is still running.
Idle sensiti̲vity **(Low / High)**	Drag slider to select this application's idle time before Windows will make CPU resources available to other programs.
Other **F̲ast pasting**	Select to use a faster paste method for this application.
Windows shortcut k̲eys	Select keys to reserve for Windows use when you use this application.

Select Text in a Document

Selects text prior to applying commands such as Cut and Copy.

Using a Windows Application

- Drag mouse through . . . . **text**
  to select.
  Windows highlights selected text.

To cancel text selection:

- Click anywhere in . . . . **document workspace**

Using an MS-DOS Application

1 Run MS-DOS application in a window (page 79).

2 Click application's . . . . **control symbol**

3 Point to . . . . **Edit** ▶

4 Click . . . . **Mark**

5 Drag mouse through . . . . **text**
  to select.
  Windows highlights selected text.

To cancel text selection:

- Press . . . . Esc

Cut or Copy Data in Document to Clipboard

NOTE: Data placed in Clipboard replaces existing Clipboard data.

From a Windows Application

1 Select data to cut or copy.

> *NOTE: See **Select Text in a Document**, page 104, for information about selecting text. You can also cut or copy graphic data to Clipboard.*

2 Click . . . . **Edit**

OR

Right-click . . . . *selection*

3 Click . . . . **Cut**
to move selection to Clipboard.

OR

Click . . . . **Copy**
to copy selection to Clipboard.

From an MS-DOS Application

1 Select text (page 104) to copy.

> *NOTE: Cut is not an option from MS-DOS applications.*

2 Click application's . . . . *control symbol*

3 Point to . . . . **Edit** ▶

4 Click . . . . **Copy**

Copy Screen Image to Clipboard

NOTE: Data placed in Clipboard replaces existing Clipboard data.

Entire Screen

- Press .... `Prnt Scrn`

Active Window

1 If image is an MS-DOS application, run MS-DOS application in a window (page 79).

2 Select window to copy.

3 Press .... `Alt` + `Prnt Scrn`

Create Scrap Documents

Creates new documents (scraps) from selected data in an open document.

NOTE: You may only create scrap documents from applications that support drag and drop functions for OLE, such as WordPad.

1 Select desired text or graphic.

2 Drag .... *selection*
  onto .... *destination folder*
  NOTE: Destination folder can be a window, icon or the desktop.

Paste Data from Clipboard into Document

NOTE: Data must be appropriate for the receiving application.

Into a Windows Application

• Run or select . . . . *application that will receive data*

By Right-Clicking

a Right-click . . . . *workspace* where data will be pasted.

b Click . . . . <u>P</u>aste

Using Menu

a Click . . . . *workspace* where data will be pasted.

b Click . . . . <u>E</u>dit, <u>P</u>aste

Into an MS-DOS Application

1 Run MS-DOS application in a window (page 79).

2 Position cursor in . . . . *workspace* where text will be pasted.

3 Click application's . . . . *control symbol*

4 Point to . . . . <u>E</u>dit ▶

5 Click . . . . <u>P</u>aste

Paste Data into Document as an OLE Object

*Pastes data from Clipboard as an embedded or linked object into current document. An **object** is a collection of information created with an OLE **object application**, such as Paint, that you can paste into a **container application**, such as WordPad.*

1 Make sure data has been copied to Clipboard from an OLE object application such as Paint.

— FROM APPLICATION TO RECEIVE OBJECT —

2 Click .... *workspace*
where data will be pasted.

3 Click .... **Edit, Paste Special...**

4 Select .... ○ **Paste**
to paste data as an embedded object.

OR

Select .... ○ **Paste Link**
to paste data as a linked object.

IMPORTANT: *If the Paste and Paste Link options are ghosted, the container application does not recognize the data in the Clipboard as an object. If Paste Link is ghosted and you want to create a link to an object, see **Insert Existing File as Linked OLE Object in Document**, page 111.*

5 Select format of object in .... **As:** list box

To display object as an icon:

• Select .... ☐ **Display As Icon**

6 Click .... [OK]

Insert New Embedded OLE Object in Document

Inserts a copy of data as an embedded object into current document. An **object** *is a collection of information created with an OLE* **object application**, *such as Paint, that you can embed into a* **container application**, *such as WordPad.*

— *FROM APPLICATION THAT WILL CONTAIN THE OBJECT* —

1 Click . . . . ***workspace***
   where object will be inserted.
2 Click . . . . **I̲nsert, O̲bject...**

> NOTE: *This procedure shows menu commands using WordPad.*
> *Command names depend on the application.*

3 Select . . . . ○ **Create N̲ew**
4 Select object type to create in . . . . **Object T̲ype:** list box

To display object as an icon:

• Select . . . . ☐ **D̲isplay As Icon**
5 Click . . . . | OK |

If object workspace appears in document:
The container application, such as Wordpad, now provides menus and tools from the object application, such as Paint.

a Use tools provided to create the object in-place.

b Click . . . . ***document workspace***
   to deselect object and return to normal editing.
   Menus and tools from the container application reappear.

If object appears as an icon:
Object application opens in a separate window and icon appears ghosted in the container application.

a Use tools provided to create the object.

b Click . . . . **F̲ile, Ex̲it & Return to Document**

c Click . . . . ***document workspace***
   to deselect object and return to normal editing.

Insert Existing File as Embedded OLE Object in Document

*Inserts a copy of existing file as an embedded object into current document.
An **object** is a collection of information created with an OLE **object
application**, such as Paint, that you can embed into a **container application**,
such as WordPad.*

— FROM APPLICATION TO RECEIVE OBJECT —

1 Click .... ***workspace***
   where object will be inserted.

2 Click .... Insert, Object...
   *NOTE: This procedure shows menu commands using WordPad.
   Command names depend on the application.*

3 Select .... ○ **Create from File**

4 Type path and file name in .... **File:** ⬜

   OR

   a Click .... ⬜ Browse...

   b Use the common dialog box to insert the file (page 55).

To display object as an icon:

   • Select .... ⬜ **Display As Icon**

5 Click .... ⬜ OK
   The object or object icon appears in the document.

6 Click .... ***document workspace***
   to deselect object and return to normal editing.
   *(Also see **Edit Embedded and Linked OLE Objects**, page 112.)*

Insert Existing File as Linked OLE Object in Document

*Inserts a link to an existing file as a linked object into current document. An **object** is a collection of information created with an OLE **object application**, such as Paint, that you can embed into a **container application**, such as WordPad. Changes made to the source object will automatically change the object in the document and other documents to which the object is linked.*

— FROM APPLICATION TO RECEIVE OBJECT —

1 Click . . . . ***workspace***
where linked object will be inserted.

2 Click . . . . **I**nsert, **O**bject...
   NOTE: *This procedure shows menu commands using WordPad.*
           Command names depend on the application.

3 Select . . . . ○ **Create from F**ile

4 Type path and file name in . . . . **Fil**e: `[      ]`

   OR

   a Click . . . . `Browse...`

   b Use the common dialog box to insert the file (page 55).

5 Select . . . . ☐ **L**ink

To display object as an icon:

   • Select . . . . ☐ **D**isplay As Icon

6 Click . . . . `OK`
   The object or object icon appears in the document.

7 Click . . . . ***document workspace***
to deselect object and return to normal editing.
   *(Also see **Edit Embedded and Linked OLE Objects**, page 112.)*

Edit Embedded and Linked OLE Objects

*NOTE: If the object was created on another computer, you can edit it only
if the same object application exists locally.*

Appearing as Data

— FROM APPLICATION CONTAINING THE OBJECT —

1   Double-click . . . . **embedded object**
Tools and menus for the object application appear in
place of container application menus and tools.

   OR

   Double-click . . . .**linked object**
The object application opens displaying the object.

2   Edit . . . . **object as desired**
If editing a linked object:

   a   Save changes made to object.

   b   Exit object application.

3   Click . . . . **document workspace**
to deselect object and return to normal editing.

Appearing as an Icon

— FROM APPLICATION CONTAINING THE OBJECT —

1   Double-click . . . . **embedded or linked object icon**
The object application opens displaying the object.

2   Edit . . . . **object as desired**
If editing a linked object:

   •   Save changes made to object.

3   Exit object application.

4   Click . . . . **document workspace**
to deselect object and return to normal editing.

Change How Linked OLE Objects are Updated

— FROM APPLICATION CONTAINING OBJECTS —

1 Click . . . . **E̲dit, Lin̲ks...**

2 Select link to change in . . . . **Li̲nks:** list box

3 Select . . . . ◯ **A̲utomatic**

 OR

 Select . . . . ◯ **M̲anual**

4 Click . . . . | Close |

Update a Manually Linked OLE Object

— FROM APPLICATION CONTAINING OBJECTS —

1 Click . . . . **E̲dit, Lin̲ks...**

2 Select link to update in . . . . **Li̲nks:** list box

3 Click . . . . | U̲pdate Now |

4 Click . . . . | Close |

Copy Embedded or Linked OLE Object

— FROM APPLICATION CONTAINING THE OBJECT —

1 Click . . . . *object to copy*

2 Click . . . . **E̲dit, C̲opy**

3 Open . . . . *application to receive copy*

NOTE: *Application must support object linking and embedding.
You can also copy the object to the same application.*

4 Click . . . . **workspace**
where object will be pasted.

5 Click . . . . **E̲dit, P̲aste**

Break Link to an OLE Object

— FROM APPLICATION CONTAINING THE OBJECT —

1 Click . . . . *linked object to break*

2 Click . . . . **E̲dit, Lin̲ks...**
Windows highlights selected object in Links list.

3 Click . . . . | Break Link |

4 Click . . . . | Yes |

5 Click . . . . | Close |

Data remains in document.

Change Link to an OLE Object

— FROM APPLICATION CONTAINING THE OBJECT —

1 Click . . . . *linked object to change or fix*

2 Click . . . . **Edit, Links...**
Windows highlights selected object in Links list.

3 Click . . . . Change Source...

4 Use the common dialog box to open new source
file for the link (page 55).

5 Click . . . . Close

Delete an OLE Object

— FROM APPLICATION CONTAINING THE OBJECT —

1 Click . . . . *object to delete*

2 Click . . . . **Edit, Clear**

OR

Press . . . . Del

Change Display of Embedded or Linked OLE Object

— FROM APPLICATION CONTAINING THE OBJECT —

1 Right-click . . . . *object to change*

2 Click . . . . **Object Properties**

FROM VIEW

3 Select . . . . ◯ **Display as editable information**

OR

Select . . . . ◯ **Display as icon**

To change icon:

a Click . . . . | Change Icon... |

b Select . . . . ◯ **Current**
to insert current icon in document.

OR

Select . . . . ◯ **Default**
to insert object application's default icon.

OR

1. Select . . . . ◯ **From File**

2. Select desired icon in . . . . **From File:** list box

   OR

   a. Click . . . . | Browse... |

   b. Use the common dialog box to
      open new file for the icon (page 55).

   c. Select desired icon in . . . . **From File:** list box

c Click . . . . | OK |

4 Click . . . . | OK |

Add Network Components

Adds network clients, adapters, protocols and services.

1 Click . . . . 🏢 **Start**

2 Point to . . . . 🗔 **Settings** ▶

3 Click . . . . 🖾 **Control Panel**

4 Double-click . . . .
 Network

| FROM **CONFIGURATION** |

5 Click . . . . | Add... |

6 Select component type to install in . . . . list box
Windows describes selected component below list box.

7 Click . . . . | Add... |

8 Select manufacturer for component
 to install in . . . . **Manufacturers:** list box

9 Select item to install in . . . . list box
 for selected manufacturer.

10 Click . . . . | OK |

11 Click . . . . | OK |

Remove Network Components

Removes installed network clients, adapters, protocols and services.

1 Click . . . . 🏁 **Start**

2 Point to . . . . 🛠 **Settings** ▶

3 Click . . . . 📁 **Control Panel**

4 Double-click . . . . 🖥
                                                               Network

> **FROM CONFIGURATION**

5 Select component to remove in . . . . list box

6 Click . . . . | Remove |

7 Click . . . . | OK |

Set File and Printer Sharing

Lets you share or end sharing of your folders and printers with others on a network.

1 Click . . . . 🏁 **Start**

2 Point to . . . . 🛠 **Settings** ▶

3 Click . . . . 📁 **Control Panel**

4 Double-click . . . . 🖥
                                                               Network

> **FROM CONFIGURATION**

5 Click . . . . | File and Print Sharing... |

6 Select or deselect . . . . ☐ **I want to be able to give others access to my files.**

7 Select or deselect . . . . ☐ **I want to be able to allow others to print to my printer(s).**

8 Click . . . . | OK |

9 Click . . . . | OK |

Change Passwords

Changes Windows and other network passwords for the current user.

1 Click . . . . `🏴 Start`

2 Point to . . . . `🔧 Settings ▶`

3 Click . . . . `📹 Control Panel`

4 Double-click . . . . `🔑`
Passwords

> *FROM CHANGE PASSWORDS*

To change Windows password:

- Click . . . . `Change Windows Password...`

  If prompted to also change other password(s):

  NOTE: *Windows will set the password(s) you select to match your Windows password.*

  1. Select password(s) to change in . . . . list box
  2. Click . . . . `OK`

OR

To change other password:

a Click . . . . `Change Other Passwords...`

b Select password to change in . . . . list box

c Click . . . . `Change...`

5 Type old password in . . . . **Old password:** `☐`

6 Type new password in . . . . **New password:** `☐`

7 Type password again in . . **Confirm new password:** `☐`

8 Click . . . . `OK`

9 Click . . . . `OK`

10 Click . . . . `Close`

Set Windows Logon Options

1 Click . . . . 🏴 **Start**

2 Point to . . . . 📑 **Settings** ▶

3 Click . . . . 📺 **Control Panel**

4 Double-click . . . . 💻💻

Network

FROM CONFIGURATION

To set Windows to log on to a Windows NT domain:

NOTE: This option requires that a user account has been created for you by your network administrator. A Windows NT server will then authenticate your password when you log on to Windows.

a Select **Client for Microsoft Networks** in . . . . list box

NOTE: If this component is not available, you must add it (page 117).

b Click . . . . | Properties |

c Select . . . . □ **Log on to Window NT domain**

d Type domain name in . . . **Windows NT domain:** [ ]

NOTE: Your network administrator must provide this name.

To set connection type when you log on to Windows:

● Select . . . . ○ **Quick logon**

OR

Select . . . . ○ **Logon and restore network connections**

5 Click . . . . | OK |

6 Click . . . . | OK |

Set Access Control of Shared Resources

Sets share-level or user-level control of your resources on a network.

1 Click .... `🏮 Start`

2 Point to .... 🏭 **Settings ▶**

3 Click .... 🗀 **Control Panel**

4 Double-click .... 🖥️

Network

┌─────── FROM ACCESS CONTROL ───────┐

5 Select .... ◯ **Share-level access control**

OR

Select .... ◯ **User-level access control**

6 Type domain or computer
name in ... **Obtain list of users and groups from:** ▭
NOTE: The Network administrator must provide this name.

7 Click .... `OK`

8 Click .... `OK`

Set Your Computer Name and Workgroup

1 Click . . . . **Start**

2 Point to . . . . **Settings** ▶

3 Click . . . . **Control Panel**

4 Double-click . . . .

Network

FROM *IDENTIFICATION*

5 Type computer name in . . . . **Computer name:** [   ]

CAUTION: *This name must be different from any other computer name on the network. The name can have up to 15 characters, but no spaces.*

6 Type your workgroup name in . . . . **Workgroup:** [   ]

NOTE: *This name identifies an existing group of computers to which you are connected. You can also create a new workgroup by typing its name in this box. The name can have up to 15 characters.*

7 Type computer description in . . . . **Description:** [   ]

8 Click . . . . [OK]

Enable Remote Administration of Your Computer

Lets others manage resources on your computer from other computers. For example, with this setting enabled, a user can run Net Watcher from a remote computer and add or remove shared resources on this computer.

1 Click . . . .　**Start**

2 Point to . . . .　**Settings** ▶

3 Click . . . .　**Control Panel**

4 Double-click . . . .　
Passwords

| FROM REMOTE ADMINISTRATION |

5 Select . . . ☐ **Enable Remote Administration on this server**

Set Share-Level Security

a Type password in . . . .　**Password:** ☐

b Type password again in . . . **Confirm password:** ☐

Set User-Level Security

To add a user or group to Administrators list:

a Click . . . .　**Add...**

b Select group or user to add in . . . .　**Name:** list box
   *NOTE: You can press **Ctrl** and click to select multiple items.*

c Click . . . .　**Add ->**

d Click . . . .　**OK**

To remove a user or group in Administrators list:

a Select user or group to remove in . . **Administrators:** list box

b Click . . . .　**Remove...**

6 Click . . . .　**OK**

Set User Profiles for Your Computer

1 Click .... 🏁 Start

2 Point to .... 🗗 <u>S</u>ettings ▶

3 Click .... 🖳 <u>C</u>ontrol Panel

4 Double-click .... 🔑
Passwords

FROM *USER PROFILES*

5 Select .. ◯ **All <u>u</u>sers of this PC use the same preferences
and desktop settings.**

OR

Select .... ◯ **Users can <u>c</u>ustomize their preferences
and desktop settings.**

To change user profile settings:

a Select or deselect ...... ☐ **Include <u>d</u>esktop icons and
Network Neighborhood
contents in user settings.**

b Select or deselect .... ☐ **Include <u>S</u>tart Menu and
Program groups in
user settings.**

6 Click .... | OK |

Log On to Windows

Windows will prompt you for a user name and password in the following cases:

- *You have set Windows to support user profiles so each user can personalize his or her environment.*
- *You are connected to a network.*

— *FROM WELCOME TO WINDOWS OR*
ENTER NETWORK PASSWORD DIALOG BOX —

1 Type your password in . . . . **Password:** [　　　　]

2 Type your user name in . . . . **User name:** [　　　　]

> *NOTE: Windows maintains security privileges and other settings for each user account.*

To log onto a Windows NT or NetWare network:

- Type domain name in . . . . **Domain:** [　　　　]

   OR

   Type login server name in . . . . . . **Login Server:** [　　　　]

> *NOTE: These names indicate the computer containing your user account. Your network administrator can set or redefine these identifiers.*

To start Windows without logging on to network:

- Click . . . . [Cancel]

3 Click . . . . [OK]

> *NOTE: When logging on for the first time, Windows will display an* **Enter Network Password** *dialog box for each network to which you are connected. If you use the same user name and password (recommended) for each network, only one logon dialog box will appear the next time you start Windows.*

Shut Down, Log On or Restart Windows

1 Click . . . . **▦ Start**

2 Click . . . . **▣ Sh<u>u</u>t Down...**

3 Select one option:

* Click . . . . ◯ **<u>S</u>hut down the computer?**

* Click . . . . ◯ **<u>R</u>estart the computer?**

* Click . . . . ◯ **Restart the computer in <u>M</u>S-DOS mode?**

* Click . . . . ◯ **<u>C</u>lose all programs and log on as a different user?**

4 Click . . . . | **<u>Y</u>es** |

> *CAUTION: Do not turn off your computer until Windows displays a message indicating it is safe to do so.*

Set Primary Network Logon

1 Click . . . . **▦ Start**

2 Point to . . . . **▨ <u>S</u>ettings ▶**

3 Click . . . . **▨ <u>C</u>ontrol Panel**

4 Double-click . . . . ▨
                                                          Network

FROM **CONFIGURATION**

5 Select desired network client or Windows Logon in . . **Primary Network <u>L</u>ogon:** | ▾ |

6 Click . . . . | **OK** |

Browse Network Computers

View or open all shared resources, such as folders and printers, on other network computers.

— FROM DESKTOP —

1 Double-click . . . .
Network Neighborhood

Computers in your workgroup or domain appear as icons.

To view other workgroups and domains:

a Double-click . . . .
Entire Network

b Double-click . . . . ***domain or workgroup***

2 Double-click . . . . ***computer icon***
containing the shared items to view.

3 Open shared folders (page 52) to view their contents.

If prompted to enter network password:

a Type password in . . . . **Password:** [ ]

b Select . . . ☐ **S̲ave this password in your password list**
OR

Deselect . . ☑ **S̲ave this password in your password list**

NOTE: If you select this option, you will not have to supply the password the next time you open the resource.

Find Computers on a Network

1   **a**   Click .... `🏢 Start`

     b   Point to .... `🔍 Find ▶`

     c   Click .... `💻 Computer...`

     OR   *— FROM EXPLORER WINDOW —*

     a   Click .... **Tools**

     b   Point to .... **Find ▶**

     c   Click .... **Computer...**

2   Select or type computer name in ..... **Named:** `[        ▼]`

     *NOTE: Windows stores past entries in the **Named***
             list box. If this is a new search, type the computer
             name or type the UNC path to a shared folder.

         EXAMPLES: `Server1`
                    `\\Server1\Accounting`
                    `"\\NTServer1\Design Work"`
                    Note the use of double quotes when folder or file
                    name includes spaces.

3   Click .... `Find Now`
     Found computers appear in a result list.

4   Double-click .... ***computer icon***
     in result list to open it.

Share a Folder or Drive

*Shares a folder or drive and all its contents with others on a network.
You can share a folder or drive from the **desktop**, a **folder** window, a
common dialog box, the **Find** window or the **Explorer** Contents pane.*

*NOTE: To share a folder, File and Print Sharing must be enabled.
See **Set Network Components Properties**, page 137.*

1   Right-click . . . . **drive or folder icon**
to share.

2   Click . . . . **Sharing...**

> FROM SHARING

3   Select . . . . ○ **Shared As:**

4   Type or edit share name in . . . . **Share Name:** ▢
*NOTE: This name appears when others view the folder on the network.
You can type a dollar sign ($) at the end of the share name
to hide it from browsers.*

5   Type comment in . . . . **Comment:** ▢
*NOTE: The comment appears in Details view
when others view the folder on the network.*

6   If dialog box displays Access Type and Passwords options,
see **Set Share-Level Access Rights**, page 130.

OR

If dialog box displays Name and Access Rights options,
see **Set User-Level Access Rights**, page 131.

*NOTE: The options for access rights will depend upon your current
access control setting. See **Set Access Control of Shared
Resources**, page 121.*

7   Click . . . . ▢ OK

If prompted for password confirmation:

a   Retype password(s).

b   Click . . . . ▢ OK

A 🖙 *appears below the shared folder icon.*

Set Share-Level Access Rights

NOTE: *The options for access rights will depend upon your current access control setting. See **Set Access Control of Shared Resources**, page 121.*

1   Follows steps to share a folder or drive (page 129).

OR

Follow steps to change properties of a shared folder or drive (page 133).

FROM SHARING

To set access type:

*   Select desired access type:

    Click . . . . ○ **R̲ead-Only**

    OR

    Click . . . . ○ **F̲ull**

    OR

    Click . . .   . ○ **D̲epends on Password**

To set read-only password:

*   Type password in . . . . . **R̲ead-Only Password:** ☐

To set full access password:

*   Type password in . . . . **Fu̲ll Access Password:** ☐

2   Click . . . . [OK]

3   If prompted, reenter passwords.

Set User-Level Access Rights

*NOTE: The options for access rights will depend upon your current access control setting. See **Set Access Control of Shared Resources**, page 121.*

1 Follows steps to share a folder or drive (page 129).

   OR

   Follow steps to change properties of a shared folder or drive (page 133).

FROM SHARING

To give access to a new user or group:

a Click . . . . | Add... |

b Select group or user to add in . . . . **Name:** list box

c Select rights for selected user or group:

   • Click . . . . | Read Only -> |

   • Click . . . . | Full Access -> |

   • Click . . . . | Custom -> |

d Repeat steps **b** and **c** for each user or group to add.

e Click . . . . | OK |

   If you set custom rights for a user or group:

   1. Select desired custom access rights.
      Custom Access Rights include: *Read Files, Write to Files, Create Files and Folders, Delete Files, Change File Attributes, List Files, Change Access Control*

   2. Click . . . . | OK |

To remove access for a user or group:

a Select user or group to remove in . . . . **Name:** list box

b Click . . . . | Remove... |

Continued ...

Set User-Level Access Rights (continued)

To edit access rights for a user or group:

a Select user or group to edit in . . . . **Name:** list box

b Click . . . . | Edit... |

c Select access rights for the user or group:

- Click . . . . ○ **Read-Only Access Rights**

- Click . . . . ○ **Full Access Rights**

- Click . . . . ○ **Custom Access Rights**

If you selected Custom Access Rights:

- Select desired access rights.
  ***Custom Access Rights include:** Read Files, Write to Files, Create Files and Folders, Delete Files, Change File Attributes, List Files, Change Access Control*

d Click . . . . | OK |

2 Click . . . . | OK |

Stop Sharing a Folder or Drive

*Stops sharing a folder with others on a network. You can do this from the desktop, a **folder window**, a **common dialog box**, the **Find** window or the **Explorer** Contents pane.*

1 Right-click . . . . **shared drive or folder icon**
NOTE: A ▨ below the icon indicates it is shared.

2 Click . . . . **Sharing...**

⌐ *FROM SHARING* ¬

3 Select . . . . ○ **Not Shared**

4 Click . . . . | OK |

Change Properties of a Shared Folder or Drive

*Changes share name, password, or access type for a shared folder or drive. You can do this from the **desktop**, a **folder** window, a **common dialog box**, the **Find** window or the **Explorer** Contents pane.*

1 Right-click . . . . ***shared drive or folder icon***

   NOTE: A ▶☞ *below the icon indicates it is shared.*

2 Click . . . . **Sharing...**

FROM SHARING

To change share name:

• Edit share name in . . . . **Share Name:** ☐

To change comment for share:

• Type comment in . . . . **Comment:** ☐

To change access rights:

If dialog box displays Access Type and Passwords options, see **Set Share-Level Access Rights**, page 130.

OR

If dialog box displays Name and Access Rights options, see **Set User-Level Access Rights**, page 131.

*NOTE: The options for access rights will depend upon your current access control setting. See **Set Access Control of Shared Resources**, page 121.*

3 Click . . . . [OK]

If prompted for password confirmation:

a Retype password(s).

b Click . . . . [OK]

Assign (Map) a Drive Letter to a Network Folder or Drive

Assigns a drive letter to a shared folder on another computer. Windows adds a network drive icon 🖳 for that network folder to the My Computer folder. You can then access that folder by browsing My Computer or by typing the drive letter and a colon when prompted for a path or at an MS-DOS prompt.

— FROM ANY FOLDER OR EXPLORER WINDOW —

1   Show toolbar (page 57).

2   Click **Map Network Drive** button . . . . [🖳]

To change suggested drive letter:

• Select drive letter in . . . . **Drive:** [▼]

3   Select or type path to shared folder in . . . **Path:** [▼]

   NOTE: Windows stores past connections in the Path list box.
   If this is a new connection, type the path in this format:
   \\computername\sharename
   EXAMPLE: \\Server1\Accounting

To retain drive assignment each time you log on:

• Select . . . . ☐ **Reconnect at logon**

4   Click . . . . [OK]

If prompted for password:

a   Type password in . . . . **Password:** [ ]

b   Select . . . ☐ **Save this password in your password list**
   OR
   Deselect . . ☑ **Save this password in your password list**

   NOTE: If you select this option, you will not have to
   supply a password the next time you open the resource.

c   Click . . . . [OK]

Windows opens a folder window for the mapped drive.

Disconnect Mapped Network Drive

Removes drive letter assignment to a shared network folder.

By Right-Clicking

— FROM MY COMPUTER FOLDER —

1 Right-click .... *mapped network drive icon*
to disconnect from.
NOTE: Icons for mapped network drives look like 🖥️

2 Click .... **<u>D</u>isconnect**

Using Toolbar

— FROM ANY FOLDER OR EXPLORER WINDOW —

1 Show toolbar (page 57).

2 Click **Disconnect Net Drive** button .... 🖳

3 Select network drive to disconnect from in ..... **Drive:** list box

4 Click .... | OK |

Specify a Path to a Shared Network Folder

Using UNC Path

You might use the Universal Naming Convention (UNC) path from a common dialog box or the Run dialog box.

• Type the path in this format:

\\computername\sharename\file name

> *EXAMPLE:* \\Server1\accounting\budget.doc *to access the file BUDGET.DOC in the shared ACCOUNTING folder on a computer named SERVER1.*

Using Mapped Network Drive Letter

You might use the mapped network drive letter from the MS-DOS prompt to make the network drive the current drive.

• Type drive letter followed by a colon .... *drv* 🅱️
  EXAMPLE: F:

Create a Shortcut to a Shared Network Folder

— FROM DESKTOP —

1 Double-click . . . .

Network
Neighborhood

Computers in your workgroup or domain appear as icons.

To view other workgroups and domains:

a Double-click . . . .

Entire Network

b Double-click . . . . *domain or workgroup*

2 Double-click . . . . *computer icon*
containing the shared items to view.

3 If necessary, open shared folders (page 52) to view
their contents.

4 Right-drag . . . . *shared folder or computer icon*
onto . . . . *destination folder*
NOTE: Destination folder can be a window, icon or the desktop.

5 Click . . . . **Create Shortcut(s) Here**

Set Network Components Properties

*Sets properties for installed network **clients, adapters, protocols** and **services**.*

1 Click . . . . `🏁 Start`

2 Point to . . . . `🎚️ Settings ▶`

3 Click . . . . `🗔 Control Panel`

4 Double-click . . . . 🖥️
                                                                   Network

---

┌──────── *FROM CONFIGURATION* ────────┐

5 Select desired component in . . . . list box
   Components include: *adapters, clients, protocols and services.*

6 Click . . . . `Properties`

The table below shows possible category tabs for network components.

Component	Tabs		Page
Adapter	Driver Type		138
	Bindings		138
	Advanced		139
	Resources		139
Client	General	(for Microsoft Networks)	140
		(for NetWare Networks)	140
Protocol	Advanced		141
	Bindings		141
	NetBIOS		141
	Gateway	*(TCP/IP only)* *	
	DNS Configuration	*(TCP/IP only)* *	
	WINS Configuration	*(TCP/IP only)* *	
	IP Address	*(TCP/IP only)* *	
Service	Advanced	(for File and printer sharing for Microsoft Networks)	142
	Other services *		

* *Specific settings for these items are not covered in this text.*

Continued ...

Set Properties of Network Components (continued)

Adapter — Driver Type

Driver Type	
Enhanced mode (32 bit and 16 bit) NDIS* driver*	Select to use the driver.
Real mode* (16 bit) NDIS* driver	Select to use the driver.
Real mode (16bit) ODI* driver	Select to use the driver.

NOTE: Options may vary.

Drivers* — *Define how protocols communicate with your network adapter card.*

NDIS* — *Network Device Interface Specification, a flexible standard of data exchange.*

ODI* — *Open Datalink Interface network adapter card driver.*

Real mode drivers* — *Network adapter drivers that reside in conventional memory.*

Adapter — Bindings

Bindings*	
IPX/SPX*-compatible Protocol	Select to use the protocol*.
NetBEUI*	Select to use the protocol. *(See below.)*
TCP/IP*	Select to use the protocol *(See below.)*

NOTE: Options may vary.

Bindings* — *Join an adapter with a protocol. Some adapters support the use of multiple protocols.*

Protocols* — *Define rules by which computers can exchange information over a network.*

IPX/SPX* — *Internetwork Packet Exchange, a protocol used on Novell® Netware® networks.*

NetBeui* — *NetBIOS Extended User Interface, a protocol used on Windows networks such as Windows for Workgroups and Windows NT.*

TCP/IP* — *Transmission Control Protocol/Internet Protocol, a protocol used to communicate with a collection of computers that use different operating systems, such as the Internet.*

Continued ...

Set Properties of Network Components (continued)

Adapter — Advanced

Advanced	*NOTE: Options may vary.*
Property	Select a property to set. **Advanced properties may include:** • I/O Channel Ready (16/32-bit) • Transceiver type **Dial-Up properties include:** • Prioritize Wan for IP • Record a log file • Use IP header compression • Use IPX header compression
Value/Not Present	Select appropriate value for selected property or select Not Present.

Adapter — Resources

Resources	*NOTE: Options may vary.*
Configuration type	Select a configuration type.
Interrupt (IRQ)	Select an interrupt value. *CAUTION: An incorrect value can cause the adapter and/or your computer to work improperly.*
I/O address range	Select a memory address range. *CAUTION: An incorrect memory range can cause the adapter and/or your computer to work improperly.*

Continued ...

Set Properties of Network Components (continued)

Client for Microsoft Networks — General

General	
Logon validation	
Log on to Window NT domain	Select to have a Windows NT domain server validate your password.
Windows NT domain*	Type name of computer that maintains the domain database for user-based security. (Required if you select the option above.)
Network logon options	
Quick logon	Select to reconnect to network drives when you use them.
Logon and restore network connections	Select to reconnect to network drives when you log on.

Domain* — A group of computers that share a centralized, user-based security system.

Client for NetWare Networks — General

General	
Preferred server	Type name of Netware computer to log on to.
First network drive	Type drive letter of first network connection.
Enable logon script processing	Select to run logon script at logon.

Domain* — A group of computers that share a centralized, user-based security system.

Continued ...

Set Properties of Network Components (continued)

Protocol — Advanced

Advanced	NOTE: *Options may vary.*
<u>P</u>roperty	Select a property to set. IPX/SPX properties include: • Force Even Length Packets • Frame Type • Maximum Connections • Maximum Sockets • Network Address • Source Routing NetBEUI properties include: • Maximum Sessions • NCBS
<u>V</u>alue/No<u>t</u> Present	Select appropriate value for selected property or select No<u>t</u> Present.

Protocol — Bindings

Bindings	NOTE: *Options may vary.*
Client for Microsoft Networks **Client for NetWare Networks**	Select client(s) to which to bind the protocol.
File and printer sharing for Microsoft Networks	Select to bind protocol to this service.

Protocol — NetBIOS

NetBIOS	
I want to <u>e</u>nable NetBIOS over IPX/SPX	Select to increase performance when communicating with other computers using IPX over NetBIOS, for example.

Continued ...

Set Properties of Network Components (continued)

Service — File and printer sharing for Microsoft Networks

Advanced	
Property	Select a property to set. Properties include: • Browse Master • LM Announce
Value	Select appropriate value for selected property.

Open the Printers Folder

The Printers folder stores the Add Printer program and installed printers as icons. Printer icons let you manage printer settings as well as view and manage the activities of the printer (the print queue).

1 Click . . . .

2 Point to . . . . 🐾 <u>S</u>ettings ▶

3 Click . . . . 🖨 <u>P</u>rinters

   NOTE: You can also open the Printers folder from My Computer.

Open a Print Queue

• Double-click . . . . ***printer icon***
  of active printer in clock area on taskbar.

  OR

  a Open Printers folder (above).

  b Double-click desired . . . . ***printer icon***

Change View of Items in the Printers Folder

1 Show toolbar (page 57).

2 Click desired button on toolbar:

  • **Large Icons** . . . . ▢

  • **Small Icons** . . . . ▢

  • **List** . . . . ▢

  • **Details** . . . . ▢

NOTE: Details view shows the following information about each printer:
    • Documents in the print queue.
    • Status of the printer.
    • The comment assigned to the printer by its owner.

Add a Local Printer

Sets up a printer directly connected to your computer for use on your system. After you add a printer, Windows adds a printer icon for the printer to your Printers folder. Windows then uses the printer software (the driver) to communicate with the printer. The printer icon lets you manage the printer settings and view, as well as manage, the activities of the printer (the print queue).

1   Open Printers folder (page 143).

2   Double-click . . . .

    The Add Printer Wizard appears.

    Add Printer

3   Click . . . . | Next > |

4   Select . . . .   ○ **L̲ocal printer**

    NOTE: If adding a network printer, refer to step **4**
             for **Add a Network Printer** *(page 146).*

5   Click . . . . | Next > |

6   Select make in . . . .   **M̲anufacturers:** list box

7   Select printer model in . . . .   **P̲rinters:** list box

8   Click . . . . | Next > |

    OR

    If you have a printer installation disk:

    a   Click . . . . | H̲ave Disk... |

    b   Follow screen prompts.

If prompted to keep existing driver:

    a   Select . . . . . .   ○ **K̲eep existing driver (recommended)**

        OR

        Select . . . .   ○ **R̲eplace existing driver**

    b   Click . . . . | Next > |

9   Select port for printer in . . . .   **A̲vailable ports:** list box

Continued ...

Add a Local Printer (continued)

To configure selected port:

a Click . . . . | Co̲nfigure Port... |

b Select options provided.

c Click . . . . | OK |

10 Click . . . . | Next > |

11 Type or edit name in . . . . **P̲rinter name:** | |

12 Select . . . . ○ **Y̲es**
to set printer as default.

OR

Select . . . . ○ **N̲o**

13 Click . . . . | Next > |

14 Select . . . . ○ **Y̲es (recommended)**
to print a test page now.

OR

Select . . . . ○ **N̲o**

15 Click . . . . | Finish |

Windows may prompt you for Windows setup disks.

Set Default Printer

Sets printer that Windows will use when you print a document and no other printer is specified.

1 Open Printers folder (page 143).

2 Right-click desired . . . . ***printer icon***

3 Click . . . . **Set As De̲fault**
*NOTES: If a check mark is next to the above option,
the printer is already set as the default printer.*

*To set the default printer, you can also click the printer,
then select Set As De̲fault on the F̲ile menu.*

Add a Network Printer

Sets up a shared printer on another computer for use on your system. After you add a printer, Windows adds a printer icon for the printer to your Printers folder. Windows then uses the printer software (the driver) to communicate with the printer. The printer icon lets you manage the printer settings and view the activities of the printer (the print queue).

NOTE: *Before you can add a network printer, the printer must be shared on the computer to which the printer is directly connected.*

1 Open Printers folder (page 143).

2 Double-click . . . .
The Add Printer Wizard appears.

Add Printer

3 Click . . . . Next >

4 Select . . . . ○ **Network printer**
NOTE: *If adding a local printer, refer to step **4** for **Add a Local Printer** (page 144).*

5 Click . . . . Next >

6 Type path to network
printer in . . . . **Network path or queue name** [   ]
NOTE: *Type path using* \\computername\sharename *format.*

OR

a Click . . . . Browse...

b Click . . . . ⊞
to the left of network/computer icon to show
items it contains.

c Repeat step **b** until desired shared printer appears.

d Click desired . . . . *printer icon*

e Click . . . . OK

7 Select . . . . ○ **Yes**
if you will use this printer from MS-DOS programs.

OR

Select . . . . ○ **No**

8 Click . . . . Next >

Continued ...

Add a Network Printer (continued)

To capture a printer port:

*NOTE: This option is provided if you answered Yes in step 7 on the
previous page. When you print from an MS-DOS application to
the port selected in step b, Windows captures the data and
sends it to the network printer instead.*

a Click . . . .   `Capture Printer Port...`

b Select port in . . . . **Device** `[          ▼]`

c Click . . . .   `OK`

d Click . . . .   `Next >`

If prompted to keep existing driver:

a Select . . . . . . ○ **Keep existing driver (recommended)**

OR

Select . . . . ○ **Replace existing driver**

b Click . . . .   `Next >`

9 Type or edit name in . . . . **Printer name:** `[        ]`

10 Select . . . . ○ **Yes**
to set printer as default.

OR

Select . . . . ○ **No**

11 Click . . . .   `Next >`

12 Select . . . . ○ **Yes (recommended)**
to print a test page now.

OR

Select . . . . ○ **No**

13 Click . . . .   `Finish`

Windows may prompt you for setup disks.

Delete a Printer

Removes printer icon from the Printers folder. Once deleted, you cannot print to that printer or manage its settings and activities.

1 Open Printers folder (page 143).

2 Right-click desired . . . . **printer icon**

3 Click . . . . **Delete**

4 Click . . . . | Yes |
to confirm.

   NOTE· To delete a printer, you can also click the printer, and select Delete on the File menu.

Rename a Printer

1 Open Printers folder (page 143).

2 Right-click desired . . . . **printer icon**

3 Click . . . . **Rename**
   Windows highlights the current name and a cursor appears at the end of the name.

4 Type or edit . . . . **name**
   NOTE: Press left arrow key to edit the name, or type a new one.

5 Press . . . . ⏎

   NOTE: To rename a printer, you can also click the printer, and select Rename on the File menu.

Set Printer to Work Offline

This option is available for network printers or printers added to a portable computer. Windows stores the documents you print to the offline printer in a local print queue until your computer has access to the printer.

1 Open Printers folder (page 143).

2 Right-click . . . . ***printer icon***
to set as offline.

3 Click . . . . **W̲ork Offline**

> *NOTES: A check mark next to this option indicates
> the printer is set to work offline.*
>
> *To set printer to work offline, you can also click the
> printer and select W̲ork Offline on the F̲ile menu.*

Pause or Restart Printer

From Printers Folder

1 Open Printers folder (page 143).

2 Click . . . . ***printer icon***
to pause or restart.

3 Click . . . . **F̲ile, P̲ause Printing**
to pause or restart the printer.

> *NOTE: A check mark next to this option indicates the printer is paused.*

From Print Queue

1 Open print queue (page 143).

2 Click . . . . **P̲rinter, P̲ause Printing**

> *NOTE: A check mark next to this option indicates the printer is paused.*

Set Properties for Printer

1   Open Printers folder (page 143).

2   Right-click . . . . ***printer icon***
to change.

3   Click . . . . **Properties**
*Windows displays a Properties dialog box with tabs
for categories of printer settings.*

4   Set options for your printer as desired.
*See options described under the General, Details and Paper
tabs in the tables that follow. Printer Sharing is covered on page 155.*

> *NOTE:*   *The tabs available depend on the type of printer you have.*
> **Details** — *Includes port and driver options.*
> **Device Options** — *Includes options such as printer memory that is unique to the selected printer.*
> **Fonts** — *May include TrueType font settings or cartridge options.*
> **General** — *Printer name, comment and separator page options.*
> **Graphics** — *Includes settings for how printer renders printed graphics.*
> **Paper** — *Includes paper size, location and orientation options.*
> **PostScript** — *Includes settings for postscript printers.*
> **Sharing** — *Includes options to share printer (page 155).*

5   Click . . . .   `OK`

General Properties of a Printer

General	NOTE: Your printer options may differ.
Comment	Type comment to appear with printer when other users connect to it, such as the description of printer location and time it is available.
Separator page	Select Full, Simple or None.
Browse...	Click to select a .WMF file (Windows metafile) to use as a separator page.
Print Test Page	Click to test printer.

Continued ...

Set Properties for Printer (continued)

Details Properties of a Printer

Details	NOTE: Your printer options may differ.
Print to the following port	Select port or shared printer in list.
Add Port...	Click to add a port or a shared printer.
Delete Port...	Click to delete a port.
Print using the following driver	Select driver or compatible driver in list.
New Driver...	Click to change or update driver for the printer.
Capture Printer Port...	Click to map a local port to a shared network printer.
End Capture...	Click to end capture (mapping) of a local port to a shared network printer.
Timeout settings	
Not selected	Type number of seconds to wait before Windows will report the printer is offline.
Transmission retry	Type number of seconds to wait before Windows will report the printer is not ready for the next part of the data.
Spool Settings...	Click to select spool options, such as when and how to send document to the printer, the spool data format. You can set bi-directional features for your printer here as well.
Port Settings...	Click to view or change port settings.

Continued ...

Set Properties for Printer (continued)

Paper Properties of a Printer

Paper	NOTE: *Your printer options may differ.*
Paper size	Select paper size in list.
Layout	Select how many logical pages can print on one physical page.

Orientation
  Portrait
  Landscape
  Rotated
	Select to print in tall paper orientation.
	Select to print in wide paper orientation.
	Select to rotate data (landscape only).

Paper source	Select printer's paper source in list.
Copies	Type or select number of copies for each print job.
Unprintable Area...	Click to set margins.
About	Describes printer device.
Restore Defaults	Click to restore original paper settings.

View Status of Print Jobs

Windows displays a printer icon in the clock area of the taskbar when data is being sent to a printer.

- Double-click . . . . ***printer icon***
  of active printer in clock area on taskbar.

  OR

  a Open Printers folder (page 143).

  b Double-click . . . . ***printer icon***
  containing the print job.

  Windows opens a print queue window for that printer.

Cancel or Pause a Print Job

1 Double-click . . . . ***printer icon***
  of active printer in clock area on taskbar.

  OR

  a Open Printers folder (page 143).

  b Double-click . . . . ***printer icon***
  containing the print job.

  — FROM PRINT QUEUE —

2 Right-click . . . . ***document***
  to cancel or pause in list.
  *NOTE: You can cancel or pause only your own documents
  on a network printer.*

3 Click . . . . **Cancel Printing**

  OR

  Click . . . . **Pause Printing**

  *NOTE: To cancel or pause a print job, you can also click the
  document, and select Pause Printing or Cancel Printing
  on the Document menu.*

Change Order of Documents in Print Queue

1 Double-click . . . . *printer icon*
of active printer in clock area on taskbar.

OR

   a Open Printers folder (page 143).

   b Double-click . . . . *printer icon*
      containing the print job.

— FROM PRINT QUEUE —

2 Drag desired . . . . *document icon*
onto desired . . . . *position in list*
NOTE: *You cannot move a document that is printing.*

Remove All Print Jobs from Print Queue

Removes from the print queue all documents waiting to be printed.

From Printers Folder

1 Open Printers folder (page 143).

2 Click . . . . *printer icon*
containing print jobs to remove.

3 Click . . . . **File, Purge Print Jobs**

From Print Queue

1 Open print queue (page 143).

2 Click . . . . **Printer, Purge Print Jobs**

Set Share Options for a Printer

Shares a local printer with others on a network, or modifies the settings of a shared printer.

*NOTE: To share a printer, File and Print Sharing must be enabled. See **Set File and Printer Sharing**, page 118.*

1 Open Printers folder (page 143).

2 Right-click desired .... ***printer icon***

3 Click .... **S̲haring...**

| FROM SHARING |

4 Select .... ○ **S̲hared As:**

5 Type or edit share name in .... **Share N̲ame:** ☐
  NOTE: This name appears when others view the printer on the network. You can type a dollar sign ($) at the end of the share name to hide it from browsers.

6 Type or edit comment in .... **C̲omment:** ☐
  NOTE: The comment appears in Details view when others view the printer on the network.

To set access security for shared printer:

• Type password in .... **P̲assword:** ☐
  NOTE: The Password option is available if access control is set to share-level (page 121).

OR

To give access to a new user or group:

  NOTE: The Add option is available if access control is set to user-level (page 121).

1. Click .... ⌐ Add... ⌐

2. Select group or user to add in .... **N̲ame:** list box

3. Click .... ⌐ F̲ull Access -> ⌐

4. Repeat steps **2** and **3** for each user or group to add.

5. Click .... ⌐ OK ⌐

Continued ...

Set Share Options for a Printer (continued)

To remove access for a user or group:

1. Select user or group to remove in . . . . . **Name:** list box
2. Click . . . . | Remove... |

7 Click . . . . | OK |

If prompted for password confirmation:

a Retype password(s).

b Click . . . . | OK |

A hand appears below the shared printer icon.

Stop Sharing a Printer

Stops sharing a printer with others on a network.

1 Open Printers folder (page 143).

2 Right-click . . . . **shared printer icon**
   NOTE: A hand below the icon indicates it is shared.

3 Click . . . . **Sharing...**

FROM SHARING

4 Select . . . . ◯ **Not Shared**

5 Click . . . . | OK |

Browse and Use Network Printers

— FROM DESKTOP —

1 Double-click . . . .
   Computers in your workgroup or domain appear as icons. Network Neighborhood

To view other workgroups and domains:

a Double-click . . . .

   Entire Network

b Double-click . . . . *domain or workgroup*

2 Double-click . . . . *computer icon*
   containing shared printer(s).

To open network printers print queue:

* Double-click desired . . . . *printer icon*
   NOTE: If you have not installed this printer on your computer, Windows will prompt you to set it up.

To install network printer:

Adds a printer (driver) for the network printer to your Printers folder.

a Right-click desired . . . . *printer icon*

b Click . . . . **Install...**

c Follow Add Printer Wizard prompts.

To map a printer port to network printer:

a Right-click desired . . . . *printer icon*

b Click . . . . **Capture Printer Port...**

c Select port in . . . . **Device** [＿＿＿＿｜▼]

d Select or deselect . . . . ☐ **Reconnect at logon**

e Click . . . . [**OK**]

To create a shortcut to network printer:

a Right-drag desired . . . . *printer icon*
   onto . . . . *destination folder*
   NOTE: Destination folder can be a window, icon or the desktop.

b Click . . . . **Create Shortcut(s) Here**

Print

Sends documents to default printer.

An Open Document Using Menu

1 Click . . . . <u>F</u>ile, <u>P</u>rint...

2 Set options in Print dialog box.

3 Click . . . . | OK |

A Closed Document by Dragging

1 Open folder (page 47) containing file to print.

2 Arrange desktop so that document and printer icon
(in Printers folder) or shortcut to printer is in view.

3 Drag . . . . *document icon*
onto . . . . *printer icon*

A Closed Document Using Send To Command

1 Open folder (page 47) containing document to print.

2 Right-click . . . . *document icon*

3 Point to . . . . **Se<u>n</u>d To** ▶

NOTE: *If desired printer does not appear on the Se<u>n</u>d To
menu, you can create a shortcut (page 88) to that
printer (in the SendTo folder). The printer will then
appear as an option on the Se<u>n</u>d To menu.*

4 Click . . . . *destination printer icon*

Stored Documents in Offline Print Queue

*This option is available for network printers or printers on some
portable computers.*

1 Open Printers folder (page 143).

2 Right-click . . . . *printer icon*
set as offline.

3 Click . . . . **<u>W</u>ork Offline**
to deselect the option.

Open the Fonts Folder to Display Installed Fonts

The Fonts folder displays installed TrueType fonts.

1 Click . . . . `Start`

2 Point to . . . . `Settings ▶`

3 Click . . . . `Control Panel`

4 Double-click . . . .

Fonts

Change View of Fonts in the Fonts Folder

1 Show toolbar (page 57).

2 Click desired button on toolbar:

- **Large Icons** . . . . `⊟`

- **List** . . . . `⊟`

- **Similarity** . . . . `AB AB`

  NOTE: See **List Installed Fonts by Similarity**, *page 160.*

- **Details** . . . . `▦`

  NOTE: *Details view shows the following information about each font:*
  - *Font Name*
  - *Filename*
  - *Size*
  - *Modified*

Hide Font Variations in the Fonts Folder

1 Click . . . . **View**

2 Select . . . . **Hide Variations (Bold, Italic, etc.)**

NOTE: A check mark next to the option indicates it is selected.

List Installed Fonts by Similarity

1 Open the Fonts folder (page 159).

2 Show toolbar (page 57).

3 Click **Similarity** button . . . .
Windows displays a drop-down list below the toolbar.

4 Select desired font
style in . . . . **List fonts by similarity to:**
Windows displays similarity of each font to the font you selected.

Install New Fonts

1 Open the Fonts folder (page 159).

2 Click . . . . **File, Install New Font...**

To change source drive:

- Select drive in . . . . **Drives:** `[            ▼]`

To change source folder:

a Double-click folder in . . . . **Folders:** list box

b Repeat step **a** until folder containing font files is opened.

3 Select font(s) in . . . . **List of fonts:** list box
*NOTE: See **Select Consecutive Items in a List Box**, page 29
and **Select Multiple Items in a List Box**, page 29.*

OR

Click . . . . `[ Select All ]`

To keep font files in original location:

- Deselect . . . . ☑ **Copy fonts to Fonts folder**

   *NOTE: To avoid duplicating the font files, you can deselect
   this option when the fonts exist on your hard disk.*

4 Click . . . . `[   OK   ]`
Windows adds font to Fonts folder.

Remove Installed Fonts

*Removes fonts from the install list of fonts, but this feature does not delete
font files.*

1 Open the Fonts folder (page 159).

2 Select font(s) in . . . . **Fonts folder**
to remove.
*NOTE: See **Select Consecutive Items in a List Box**, page 29
and **Select Multiple Items in a List Box**, page 29.*

3 Click . . . . **File, Delete**

OR

Press . . . . `Del`

Show or Print Font Sample

Shows typeface name, file size, version and sample of selected font in various point sizes.

1 Open the Fonts folder (page 159).

   OR

   Open folder (page 52) containing font files.
   NOTE: Font files have .TTF and .FON file name extensions.

2 Double-click . . . . ***font icon***
   to preview.

   ### To print font sample:

   a Click . . . . [<u>P</u>rint]

   b Click . . . . [OK]

3 Click . . . . [<u>D</u>one]
   to close the window.

Show Font Properties

Shows fonts from the install list of fonts, but this feature does not delete font files.

1 Open the Fonts folder (page 159).

2 Right-click desired font in . . . . ***Fonts folder***

3 Click . . . . ***P<u>r</u>operties...***
   Font properties include: Type, Location, Size, MS-DOS name, Created, Modified, Accessed, Attributes.

4 Click . . . . [OK]

Set Accessibility Properties

1 Click .... 🏁 **Start**

2 Point to .... 🎛 **Settings** ▶

3 Click .... 🗔 **Control Panel**

4 Double-click .... 🔒 *Accessibility Options*

 NOTE: If Accessibility Options icon is not visible, see **Add or Remove Windows Components** *on page 91.*

5 Set properties described in tables that follow.

Keyboard	
Use StickyKeys	Select to set Alt, Ctrl, and Shift to remain active until next key is pressed.
Settings	Click to set these StickyKeys options: • Use shortcut • Press modifier key twice to lock • Turn StickyKeys off if two keys are pressed at once • Make sounds when modifier key is processed • Show StickyKeys status on screen
Use **F**ilterKeys	Select to set Windows to ignore brief repeated keystroke or slow repeat rate.
S**e**ttings	Click to set these FilterKeys options: • Use shortcut • Ignore repeated keystrokes and Settings • Ignore quick keystrokes and slow down the repeat rate and Settings • Click and type here to test FilterKey settings • Beep when keys pressed or accepted • Show FilterKey status on screen
Use **T**oggleKeys	Select to set Windows to create sounds when keys like Num Lock, Caps Lock, and Scroll Lock are pressed.
Se**tt**ings	Click to set these ToggleKeys options: • Use shortcut

Continued ...

Set Accessibility Properties (continued)

Keyboard	*continued*
Show extra keyboard help in programs	Select to show extra help for programs that support this option.

Sound	
Use SoundSentry	Select to set Windows to display visual warnings when your computer makes a sound.
Settings	Click to set these SoundSentry options: • Warning for windowed programs • Warning for full screened text programs • Warning for full screened graphics programs
Use ShowSounds	Select to set programs to display captions and icons when the program generates sounds.

Display	
Use High Contrast	Select to increase screen readability.
Settings	Click to set these High Contrast settings: • Use shortcut • White on black • Black on white • Custom

Continued ..

Set Accessibility Properties (continued)

Mouse	
Use <u>M</u>ouseKeys	Select to use numeric keypad for mouse pointer operations.
<u>S</u>ettings	Click to set these MouseKeys options: • <u>U</u>se shortcut • <u>T</u>op speed (Pointer speed) • <u>A</u>cceleration (Pointer speed) • <u>H</u>old down Ctrl to speed up and Shift to slow down (Pointer speed) • Use MouseKeys when NumLock is O<u>n</u> or Of<u>f</u> • S<u>h</u>ow MouseKey status on screen

General	
Automatic reset **<u>T</u>urn off accessibility features after idle for *n* minutes**	Select to set idle time at which all Accessibility settings will be disabled except SerialKeys.
Notification **<u>G</u>ive warning message when turning a feature on**	Select to set this Notification option.
Make a <u>s</u>ound when turning a feature on or off	Select to set this Notification option.
SerialKey devices **S<u>u</u>pport SerialKey devices**	Select to support special input devices that can be attached to a serial port.
S<u>e</u>ttings	Click to set these SerialKeys options: • <u>S</u>erial port • <u>B</u>aud rate

Set Date and Time

- Double-click . . . . *clock on taskbar*

  OR

  a Click . . . . **🏁 Start**

  b Point to . . . . **⚙️ <u>S</u>ettings ▶**

  c Click . . . . **📷 <u>C</u>ontrol Panel**

  d Double-click . . . . **🕐**

  Date/Time

FROM DATE & TIME

To change the month:

- Select month in . . . . [▾]
  in <u>D</u>ate area.

To change the year:

- Select year in . . . . [⬍]
  in <u>D</u>ate area.

To change the day:

- Select day in . . . . *calendar*

To change the time:

- **a** Double-click time item in . . . . [⬍]
  below the clock.
  Time items include: hours, minutes, seconds, and AM/PM.

- **b** Type desired value for item.
  *NOTE: For AM/PM item, type A for AM or P for PM.
  You can also click the increment arrows to
  increase or decrease the selected value.*

Continued ...

Set Date and Time (continued)

FROM TIME ZONE

To change time zone:
- Select time zone in . . . . [＿＿＿＿＿＿ ▾]

  OR

  Click desired area on map.

To adjust clock for daylight saving time:
- Select . . . . ☐ **Automatically adjust clock for daylight saving changes**

Add New Hardware

1 Click . . . . [🏢 Start]

2 Point to . . . . 🗇 **Settings ▸**

3 Click . . . . 📟 **Control Panel**

4 Double-click . . . .

Add New
Hardware

5 Carefully follow **Add New Hardware Wizard** directions.

Set Keyboard Properties

1 Click . . . . 🏢 Start

2 Point to . . . . 🔧 <u>S</u>ettings ▶

3 Click . . . . 📺 <u>C</u>ontrol Panel

4 Double-click . . . . ⌨

Keyboard

5 Set properties described in tables that follow.

Speed	
<u>C</u>haracter repeat	
Repeat <u>d</u>elay	Select time delay before characters repeat when you hold down a key.
<u>R</u>epeat rate	Select speed at which characters repeat when you hold down a key.
Click here and hold down a key to <u>t</u>est repeat rate	Select then press key to test.
Cursor <u>b</u>link rate	Select a rate at which cursor blinks.

Continued ...

Set Keyboard Properties (continued)

Language	
Language **Layout**	Shows keyboard languages and layouts.
Add	Click to add a keyboard language.
Properties	Click to change layout of selected keyboard language.
Remove	Click to delete selected keyboard language and layout.
Set as Default	Click to use selected language and layout as default.

Switch languages
   Left Alt+Shift
   Ctrl+Shift
   None
	Select keys to switch between languages.

Enable indicator on taskbar	Select to show language keyboard indicator on taskbar. You can double-click the indicator to select a language.

General	
Keyboard type	Shows current keyboard type.
Change	Click to change current keyboard type.

Set Mail and Fax Properties

1 Click . . . . 🔡 **Start**

2 Point to . . . . 🖳 **Settings** ▶

3 Click . . . . 🖳 **Control Panel**

4 Double-click . . . .

Mail and FAX

5 Set properties described in tables that follow.

> *NOTE: If you have not set up a Microsoft Exchange profile,
> click the Add button from the General tab to start the
> Inbox Setup Wizard.*

Current Profile Properties

Services	
information service list box	Shows installed information services for the current profile. Information services you can install include: • Microsoft Fax • Microsoft Mail • Personal Address Book • Personal Information Store • The Microsoft Network Online Service • CompuServe Mail • Internet Mail
Add	Click to add an information service.
Remove	Click to remove selected information service from the current profile.
Properties	Click to set properties of selected information service.
Copy	Click to copy selected information service to another profile.
About	Click to view file information about selected information service.
Show Profiles	Click to show and select profiles set up on your computer.

Continued ...

Set Mail and Fax Properties (continued)

Delivery	
Deliver new items to the following location	Select location to store new mail items.
Secondary location	Select location to store mail items if location above is not available.
Recipient addresses are processed by these information services in the following order	Select a service in the list, then click the up and down arrows to change the order of outgoing items for that service.

Addressing	
Show this address list first	Select the default address list.
Keep personal addresses in	Select list in which to keep personal addresses.
When sending mail, check names using these address lists in the following order	Select an address book in the list, then click the up and down arrows to change the order of address book usage.
Add	Click to add an address list.
Remove	Click to remove selected address list.
Properties	Click to view information about selected address list.

Create a New Workgroup Postoffice

NOTE: Only one postoffice should be set up in a workgroup.

1 Click .... **Start**

2 Point to .... **Settings ▶**

3 Click .... **Control Panel**

4 Double-click .... Microsoft Mail Postoffice

5 Select .... ◯ **Create a new Workgroup Postoffice**

6 Click .... Next >

7 Type path to postoffice in ... **Postoffice Location:** [ ]

OR

   a Click .... Browse...

   b Use the common dialog box (page 55) to select the location.

8 Click .... Next >

Microsoft Workgroup Postoffice Admin displays location and name of postoffice.

9 Click .... Next >

10 Enter Administrator Account Details.
   Administrator Account Details include: *Name, Mailbox, Password, Phone #1, Phone #2, Office, Department, Notes*

11 Click .... OK

12 Read message about sharing the postoffice.

13 Click .... OK

Administer Existing Microsoft Postoffice

1 Click . . . . `Start`

2 Point to . . . . `Settings ▶`

3 Click . . . . `Control Panel`

4 Double-click . . . .

Microsoft Mail
Postoffice

5 Select . . . ○ **Administer an existing Workgroup Postoffice**

6 Click . . . . `Next >`
Windows displays location of postoffice in **Postoffice Location** *text box.*

7 Click . . . . `Next >`
Windows displays administrator's mailbox name in **Mailbox** *text box.*

8 Type your Mail password in . . . . **Password** `_____`

9 Click . . . . `Next >`

To add a mail user:

a Click . . . . `Add User...`

b Set options for user as desired.
  Add User settings include: *Name, Mailbox, Password,
  Phone #1, Phone #2, Office, Department, Notes*

c Click . . . . `OK`

To remove a mail user:

a Select user to remove in . . . . **Users on** list box

b Click . . . . `Remove User`

c Click . . . . `Yes`

Continued ...

Administer Existing Microsoft Postoffice (continued)

To change settings for existing mail user:

a Click .... | Details... |

b Set options for user as desired.
User settings include: _Name, _Mailbox, _Password,
Phone #_1, Phone #_2, _Office, _Department, No_tes

c Click .... | OK |

10 Click .... | Close |

Install a Modem

1 Click .... | 🏁 Start |

2 Point to .... 🗔 _Settings ▶

3 Click .... 🗔 _Control Panel

4 Double-click .... 📞
Modems

5 Carefully follow **Install New Modem** wizard directions.

OR

FROM *GENERAL*

a Click .... | _Add... |

b Carefully follow **Install New Modem** wizard directions.

NOTE: *Windows can detect your modem, or you can select
it from a list.*

Set Modem Properties

1 Click .... 🏁 **Start**

2 Point to .... 🗔 **Settings** ▶

3 Click .... 🗔 **Control Panel**

4 Double-click .... 📞

Modems

5 Set properties described in tables that follow.

General	
Add	Click to install a new modem.
Remove	Click to remove selected modem.
Properties	Click to set properties for selected modem.
	General modem properties include:
	• Port
	• Speaker volume
	• Maximum speed
	• Only connect at this speed
	Connection modem properties include:
	• Data bits
	• Parity
	• Stop bits
	• Wait for dial tone before dialing
	• Cancel the call if not connected within *n* secs
	• Disconnect a call if idle for more than *n* mins
	• Port Settings
	Use FIFO buffers (req. 16550 UART)
	Receive Buffer (Low/High)
	Transmit Buffer (Low/High)
	Defaults
	• Advanced
	Use error control, Required to connect
	Compress data, Use cellular protocol
	Use flow control, Hardware (RTS/CTS)
	Software (XON/XOFF), Modulation type,
	Extra settings, Record a log file

Continued ...

Set Modem Properties (continued)

General	continued
Dialing Properties	Lets you set dialing properties: Where I am: • I am dialing from (location) • New, Remove (location) • The area code is • I am in (country) How I dial from this location: • To access an outside line, first dial *n* for local and *n* for long distance • Dial using Calling Card • This location has call waiting. To disable it, dial *n*. The phone system at this location uses: • Tone dialing, Pulse dialing

Diagnostics	
Port Installed	Shows available communication ports and installed devices.
Driver	Click to show communication driver for selected port.
More Info	Click to view Port information: • Port • Interrupt • Address • UART • Highest Speed and Command Responses (diagnostics on selected modem).
Help	Click to start Modem Troubleshooter.

Set Mouse Properties

1 Click . . . . **Start**

2 Point to . . . . **Settings** ▶

3 Click . . . . **Control Panel**

4 Double-click . . . .

Mouse

5 Set properties described in tables that follow.

Buttons	
Button configuration **Right-handed** **Left-handed**	Select primary mouse button.
Double-click speed	Select time between sequence of clicks when double-clicking.
Test area	Double-click icon to test double-click speed.

Pointers	
Scheme	Select a saved pointers scheme.
Save As	Click to save current pointers settings as a scheme.
Delete	Click to delete selected pointers scheme.
Use Default	Click to use default pointers scheme.
Browse	Click to replace selected pointer with another pointer. (Pointers are stored in .CUR files.)

Motion	
Pointer speed	Select to change speed of pointer when moving mouse.
Show pointer trails	Select to show trail when moving mouse. Then, drag slider to adjust length of pointer trail.

Continued ...

Set Mouse Properties (continued)

General	
Name	Shows current mouse type.
Change	Click to change current mouse type.

Set Multimedia Properties

1 Click .... 🏁**Start**

2 Point to .... 🗂️ **Settings** ▶

3 Click .... 🗂️ **Control Panel**

4 Double-click ....

Multimedia

5 Set properties described in tables that follow.

Audio	
Playback	
Volume	Select volume for playback sounds.
Preferred device	Select preferred audio hardware device.
Show volume control on the taskbar	Select to enable volume control indicator on taskbar. You can click the indicator to change the volume, or double-click the indicator to open the Volume Control window if your sound card supports the feature.
Recording	
Volume	Select volume for recorded sounds.
Preferred device	Select preferred audio hardware device.
Preferred quality	Select preferred recorded sound qualities.
Customize	Click to select a sound quality or create custom recording sound formats.
Use preferred devices only	Select to ensure programs use only the preferred sound device.

Continued ...

Set Multimedia Properties (continued)

MIDI	
Single instrument	Select a specific MIDI instrument.
Custom configuration	Select to use default or a custom MIDI configuration.
MIDI Scheme	Select desire MIDI instrument configuration.
Configure	Click to create or modify a MIDI scheme.
Add New Instrument	Click to add driver for a new MIDI instrument.

CD Music	
Volume settings	
CD-ROM drive	Select drive letter to use as default CD player.
Headphone	Select headphone volume for selected CD-ROM drive.

Video	
Show video in	
Window	Select to set size of window in which you will show video clips.
Full screen	Select to have video clips fill entire screen.

Advanced	
Multimedia devices	Select plus sign (+) of multimedia device category to view or edit, then click the device.
Properties	Click to edit properties for selected multimedia device.

Install PC Card (PCMCIA) Support or Set PC Card Properties

1 Click . . . . `🏁 Start`

2 Point to . . . . 🦋 **Settings** ▶

3 Click . . . . 🖼️ **Control Panel**

4 Double-click . . . . 🔲

PC Card
(PCMCIA)

5 Follow PC Card (PCMCIA) wizard prompts.

NOTE: The PC Card (PCMCIA) wizard appears automatically if this feature has not been installed.

OR

Set properties described in tables that follow.

Socket Status	
**List of PC cards in available sockets ** *	View status of cards in this list or select PC card to remove.
S̲top	Safely stops selected PC card.
S̲how control on taskbar	Select to enable the option.
D̲isplay warning if card is removed before it is stopped.	Select to enable the option.

* NOTE: To change the number of available sockets:
Use Notepad to edit the last two lines of C:\CONFIG.SYS to read:
DEVICE=c:\windows\system\CSMAPPER.SYS
DEVICE=c:\windows\system\CARDDRV.EXE /SLOT=n
*where **n** is the number of sockets. Then save and restart.*

Global Settings	

Card services shared memory
    Automatic selection
    Start
    End
    Length
	Select to enable the option or deselect and type shared memory address in each text box.

Disable PC card sound effects	Select to enable the option.

Set Up Data Source Drivers

Sets up Open Database Connectivity (ODBC) drivers (drivers that enable access to data sources) for use by Windows applications, such as Microsoft Excel, that are designed to utilize ODBC data sources.

1 Click . . . . |🏁 Start|

2 Point to . . . . 📁 <u>S</u>ettings ▶

3 Click . . . . 🖥 **Control Panel**

4 Double-click . . . . 🖥️
                                                                        ODBC

5 Set up data sources and drivers as described below.

<u>D</u>ata Sources (Driver)	Lists installed data source drivers.
<u>S</u>etup	Click to set up selected data source.
De<u>l</u>ete	Click to delete selected data source.
<u>A</u>dd	Click to add a new data source.
D<u>r</u>ivers	Click to add, delete or display information about an ODBC driver.
<u>O</u>ptions	Click to set ODBC default options.

Set Regional Properties

1 Click . . . . 🏁 **Start**

2 Point to . . . . 🔧 **Settings** ▶

3 Click . . . . 🖼 **Control Panel**

4 Double-click . . . . ⬤ Regional Settings

5 Set properties described in tables that follow.

Regional Settings	
Country and region list	Select region in list to use.
Map	Click region in map to use.

Number	
Appearance samples	Shows result of settings after clicking Apply.
Decimal symbol	Select desired decimal symbol.
No. of digits after decimal	Select number of digits.
Digit grouping symbol	Select symbol that groups digits in large numbers.
No. of digits in group	Select number of digits between digit grouping symbols.
Negative sign symbol	Select symbol that shows negative values.
Negative number format	Select format that shows negative values.
Display leading zeroes	Select a format to show or hide leading zeros before decimal symbol in decimal values.
Measurement system	Select a measurement system.
List separator	Select symbol used to separate list items.

Continued ...

Set Regional Properties (continued)

Currency	
Appearance samples	Shows results of settings after clicking Apply.
Currency symbol	Select a currency symbol.
Position of currency symbol	Select display position of currency symbol.
Negative number format	Select format that shows negative values.
Decimal symbol	Select desired decimal symbol.
No. of digits after decimal	Select desired number of digits to show after decimal symbol.
Digit grouping symbol	Select symbol that groups digits in large numbers.
No. of digits in group	Select number of digits between digit grouping symbols.

Time	
Appearance	
Time sample	Shows results of settings after clicking Apply.
Time style	Select time format.
Time separator	Select hour, minute, second separator symbol.
AM symbol	Select before noon symbol.
PM symbol	Select afternoon symbol.

Continued ...

Set Regional Properties (continued)

Date	
Calendar type	Select desired calendar type.
Short date	
Short date sample	Shows result of settings after clicking Apply.
Short date style	Select desired short date format.
Date separator	Select desired short date separator.
Long date	
Long date sample	Shows result of setting after clicking Apply.
Long date style	Select desired long date format.

Set Sound Properties

1 Click . . . .

2 Point to . . . . 🐾 **Se̲ttings** ▶

3 Click . . . . 🗔 **Control Panel**

4 Double-click . . . .

Sounds

5 Set properties described in table that follows.

Sounds	
Ev̲ents	Select event to assign a sound to.
Sound	
N̲ame	Select .WAV file to assign to selected event.
B̲rowse	Click to select other .WAV files to assign to selected event.
D̲etails	Click to display properties of .WAV file in Name list.
Preview button ▶	Click to preview sound for selected event.
Sc̲hemes	Select a named set of events and the sounds assigned to them.
S̲ave As	Click to save current event assignments to a named scheme.
D̲elete	Click to delete selected scheme.

Set System Properties

Lets you view general information about your system, manage devices (enable, disable and set device properties), set up hardware profiles, and set performance options such as use of virtual memory.

1 a Right-click . . . . My Computer

   b Click . . . . **Properties...**

   OR

   a Click . . . . |▒▒ Start|

   b Point to . . . . **Settings ▶**

   c Click . . . . **Control Panel**

   d Double-click . . . . System

2 Set or view properties described in tables that follow.

   CAUTION: You should not change a system setting unless you completely understand the effect of the change.

General	
System	Shows the version of Windows that is running.
Registered to	Shows name of registered user.
Computer	Shows computer processor and total memory.

Device Manager	
View devices by type	Select to list devices under their categories.
View devices by connection	Select to list devices under the hardware to which they are connected.
hardware list	Select plus sign (+) of device category or connection to view or edit, then click the device to select it.

Continued ...

Set System Properties (continued)

Device Manager	continued
Properties *NOTE: Depending on the device, other property tabs may be available.*	Click to change or view properties of selected device. **General properties include:** • Information about the device • Device usage — select hardware profile for which the device can be enabled or disabled. **Driver properties may include:** • Driver files, File details, Change Driver **Resource properties may include:** • Resource settings (such as IRQ/Memory Address) • Use automatic settings • Change Setting • Conflicting device list
Refresh	Click to update list to show recent changes.
Remove	Click to remove selected device in hardware list.
Print	Click to print summary of hardware devices and their properties.

Hardware Profiles	
profiles list	Shows hardware profiles (hardware device settings) for your computer.
Copy	Click to copy selected profile to a new hardware profile. You can then select or deselect hardware devices for use with the profile.
Rename	Click to rename selected profile.
Delete	Click to delete selected profile.

Continued ...

Set System Properties (continued)

Performance	
Performance status	
Memory	Shows total RAM for your computer.
System Resources	Shows percentage of free system resources.
File System	Shows type of file system in use.
Virtual Memory	Shows type of virtual memory in use.
Disk Compression	Shows type of disk compression in use.
PC Cards (PCMCIA)	Shows information about PC Cards in use.
Advanced settings	
File System	Click to set or view: Hard Disk properties • Typical role of this machine (Desktop computer, Mobile or docking system, Network server) • Read-ahead optimization CD-ROM properties • Supplemental cache size • Optimize access pattern for (speed of CD-ROM) Troubleshooting settings • Disable listed settings.
Graphics	Click to set graphics hardware acceleration.
Virtual Memory	Click to set these virtual memory properties: • Let Windows manage my virtual memory settings (recommended) • Let me specify my own virtual memory settings Hard disk Minimum Maximum Disable virtual memory (not recommended)

Briefcase

Synchronizes files you work with on different computers.

Briefcase Icon, Folder and Update Prompt

Location If you installed Briefcase, the My Briefcase icon will appear on the desktop.

> *NOTE: If you did not install **Briefcase**, see **Add or Remove Windows Components**, page 91.*

What You Can Do with Briefcase

- Create additional Briefcase folders to which you can copy files you want to work with on another computer.
- Move a Briefcase folder and its contents to another computer.
- Synchronize (update) files in a Briefcase or the original files.
- Display status of synchronization in Details view.
- Split synchronized files so they can be worked with separately.

Briefcase (continued)

Create New Briefcase

1 Right-click empty area on ...... *desktop or folder window*

2 Point to .... **New** ▶

3 Click .... **Briefcase**

Briefcase Menu Commands

NOTE: Briefcase folder windows also contain menus common to all folders in Windows. Those menu items are not covered here.

Briefcase	
Update All...	Updates all files in the Briefcase folder.
Update Selection	Updates selected files in the Briefcase folder.
Split From Original	Splits selected file so it can be worked with separately.

Briefcase Tip—Keep Your Briefcase on a Floppy Disk

FROM YOUR MAIN COMPUTER
- Move the Briefcase onto a floppy disk.
- Drag the files you want to take on the road onto this Briefcase.
  NOTE: If you do additional work on these files from your main computer, open the Briefcase on the floppy disk and select the Update All command.

WHEN ON THE ROAD
- Open the Briefcase on the floppy disk
- Drag the files to a folder on your other computer's hard disk. Leave the Briefcase on the floppy disk.

When you have finished working with these files:
- Open the Briefcase on the floppy disk.
- Select the Update All command.

WHEN YOU GET BACK TO YOUR MAIN COMPUTER
- Open the Briefcase on the floppy disk.
- Select the Update All command.

Windows Applications

191

Calculator

Performs standard and advanced calculations.

Standard Calculator

Scientific Calculator

Location   📇Start Programs, Accessories

> *NOTE: If you did not install **Calculator**, see **Add or Remove Windows Components**, page 91.*

Calculator (continued)

What You Can Do with Calculator

- Perform calculations.
- Store values in memory.
- Copy and paste data to and from the Clipboard.
- Choose between Standard and Scientific calculators.

Calculator Menu Commands

Edit	
Copy	Copies displayed number to the Clipboard.
Paste	Inserts a number or equation from the Clipboard to the Calculator's display.

View	
Scientific	Opens the Scientific Calculator.
Standard	Opens the Standard Calculator.

Calculator (continued)

Basic Calculator Functions
FOR STANDARD AND SCIENTIFIC CALCULATORS

Function	Button	Key
Add	+	+
Calculate	=	= or Enter
Calculate reciprocal	1/x	R
Change sign of number	+ —	F9
Clear displayed number or function	CE	Del
Clear calculator	C	Esc
Decimal point	.	. or ,
Delete last number entered	BACK	Bksp
Divide	/	/
Multiply	*	*
Percentage (calculate)*	%	%
Square root of displayed number*	sqrt	@
Subtract	—	—

Memory Functions	Button	Key
Add displayed number to memory value ...	M+	Ctrl + P
Clear memory	MC	Ctrl + L
Display contents of memory	MR	Ctrl + R
Store number in memory	MS	Ctrl + M

* Applies only to Standard Calculator.

Calculator (continued)

Scientific Calculator Functions

Scientific Functions		
Number Systems	**Button**	**Key**
Decimal	Dec	F6
Sets trigonometric input to: (when in Decimal mode)		
degrees	Deg	F2
gradients	Grad	F4
radians	Rad	F3
Binary	Bin	F8
Hexadecimal	Hex	F5
Octal	Oct	F7
Displays representation of number in: (when in Binary, Hexadecimal or Octal mode)		
Byte (lower 8 bits)	Byte	F4
Dword (full 32 bits)	Dword	F2
Word (lower 16 bits)	Word	F3
Logical Operators	**Button**	**Key**
Bit shift (left one bit)	Lsh	<
Bit shift inverse (right one bit)	Inv + Lsh	i + <
Calculate bitwise inverse	Not	~
Calculate bitwise exclusive OR	Xor	^
Calculate bitwise OR	Or	I
Calculate bitwise AND	And	&
Displays remainder of division operation . . .	Mod	%
Integer	Int	;
Integer (fraction)	Inv + Int	i + ;
Level of calculation ( )	( )	( )

Calculator (continued)

Scientific Calculator Functions

Scientific Functions		
Statistical Functions	**Button**	**Key**
Calculate:		
mean	Ave	Ctrl + A
mean of the squares	Inv + Ave	i + Ctrl + A
standard deviation (pop. = n)	Inv + s	i + Ctrl + D
standard deviation (pop. = $n - 1$)	s	Ctrl + D
sum	Sum	Ctrl + T
sum of squares	Inv + Sum	i + Ctrl + T
Open Statistics Box:	Sta	Ctrl + S
change number in calculator display to selected number	LOAD	Alt + L
delete all numbers	CAD	Alt + A
delete currently selected number	CD	Alt + C
enter number displayed from calculator . .	Dat	Insert
switch to main calculator (and retain Statistic Box entries)	RET	Alt + R

Calculator (continued)

Other Scientific Functions

Functions	Button	Key
Calculate:		
10 raised to x^n power	Inv + log	i + l
arc cosine	Inv + cos	i + o
arc sine	Inv + sin	i + s
arc tangent	Inv + tan	i + t
arc hyperbolic cosine	Inv + Hyp + cos	i + h + o
arc hyperbolic sine	Inv + Hyp + sin	i + h + s
arc hyperbolic tangent	Inv + Hyp + tan	i + h + t
common logarithm (base 10)	log	l
cosine	cos	o
cube	x^3	#
cube root	Inv + x^3	i + #
e raised to x^n power	Inv + ln	i + n
factorial	n!	!
hyperbolic cosine	Hyp + cos	h + o
hyperbolic sine	Hyp + sin	h + s
hyperbolic tangent	Hyp + tan	h + t
natural logarithm (base e)	ln	n
sine	sin	s
square	x^2	@
square root	Inv + x^2	i + @
tangent	tan	t
x raised to y^n power	x^y	y
y^n root of x	Inv + x^y	i + y
Degree-minute-second format	dms	m
Inverse function (set function to)	Inv	i
Pi (input value of)	PI	p
Pi times 2 (input value of)	Inv + PI	i + p
Scientific notation (set entry mode to)	Exp	x
Scientific notation (toggle on and off)	F - E	v

CD Player

Plays audio compact discs. To use CD Player you must have a CD-ROM and a sound card installed.

CD Player

Location   [🎯Start]   Programs, Accessories, Multimedia

> *NOTE: If you did not install **CD Player**, see **Add or Remove Windows Components**, page 91.*

What You Can Do with CD Player

- Play audio compact discs.
- Edit and name the play list.
- Change tracks.
- Access Volume Control.
- Set random and continuous play of music.
- Select Intro Play (to preview tracks).

CD Player (continued)

CD Player Toolbar

The illustration below identifies the buttons on CD Player's toolbar.

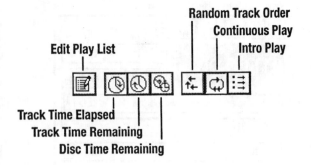

CD Player Audio Controls

The illustration below identifies CD Player's audio controls.

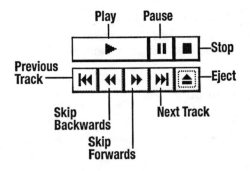

CD Player Menu Commands

Disc	
Edit Play List...	Lets you add and remove tracks to play; names tracks; name the artist and title of the audio compact disc.
Exit	Exits CD Player program.

Continued ...

CD Player (continued)

View	
Toolbar	Shows or hides the CD Player toolbar.
Disc/Track Info	Shows or hides artist, title and track information.
Status Bar	Shows or hides play and track information on status bar.
Track Time Elapsed **Track Time Remaining** **Disc Time Remaining**	Lets you select desired display option.
Volume Control	Opens Volume Control from which you can set volume options for the CD Player.

Options	
Random Order	Plays audio tracks in random order.
Continuous Play	Sets the CD Player to play audio continuously.
Intro Play	Plays beginning of each track on the CD.
Preferences	Lets you set the following options: • Stop CD playing on exit • Save settings on exit • Show tooltips • Intro play length (seconds) • Display font Small font Large font

Character Map

Lets you select and insert special characters into any Windows document.

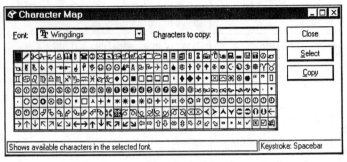

Character Map

Location   📕**Start** Programs, Accessories

> *NOTE: If you did not install **Character Map**, see **Add or Remove Windows Components**, page 91.*

What You Can Do with Character Map

- Browse installed fonts for special characters.
- Select one or more special characters and copy them into any Windows document.

Insert Special Character into Document

— FROM CHARACTER MAP —

1 Select font containing character in . . . . . **Font:** [▼]

2 If desired, point to character and press and hold left mouse button to enlarged it.

3 Double-click . . . . *character* to select it.

4 Click . . . . [Copy]

— FROM DESTINATION DOCUMENT —

5 Click . . . . **Edit**, **Paste**

Clipboard Viewer

Lets you view data stored in the Clipboard.

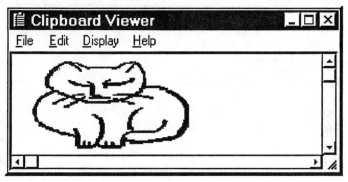

Clipboard Viewer Showing Bitmap Data

Location   [Start]   Programs, Accessories

> *NOTE: If you did not install **Clipboard Viewer**, see **Add or Remove Windows Components**, page 91.*

What You Can Do with Clipboard Viewer

- View data stored in the Clipboard.
- Save data stored in the Clipboard to a file.
- Open a saved Clipboard (.CLP) file.
- Change the format of data stored in the Clipboard.

Clipboard Viewer Menu Commands

File	
Open	Opens a saved .CLP file.
Save As	Saves the contents in the Clipboard to a file.
Exit	Exits the Clipboard Viewer program.

Continued ...

Clipboard Viewer (continued)

Edit	
Delete	Deletes the contents of Clipboard.

Display	
Auto **R**ich Text Format **T**ext **L**ocale **O**EM Text	Lets you select a format for the data in Clipboard. *NOTE: Format options will depend on the data in Clipboard.*

Dial-Up Networking

Lets you connect to local and network resources on a remote computer that is running dial-up server software. Dial-Up Networking requires a modem.

Starting a Dial-Up Networking Connection

Location   🔳Start   Programs, Accessories
OR
The My Computer folder
*NOTE: If you did not install **Dial-Up Networking**, see*
*   **Add or Remove Windows Components**, page 91.*

What You Can Do with Dial-Up Networking

- Connect to a remote computer if it is running dial-up server software such as Windows NT 3.5 Remote Access Server.
- Use shared network resources (folders and printers) as if they were part of your computer. (This requires that you have installed the same network protocols as the dial-up server.)
- Use Microsoft Exchange to exchange email with users on the remote computer and its network.

Dial-Up Networking (continued)

Dial-Up Networking Menu Commands

NOTE: The Dial-Up Network folder also contains menus common to all folders in Windows. These menu items are not covered here.

File	
Connect	Makes connection using selected connection item in Dial-Up Networking folder.

Properties	Lets you set properties for selected connection item. General properties include:
	• Phone number: Area code, Telephone number, Country code, Use country code and area code
	• Connect using: (select modem in list box)
	• Configure (modem)
	• Server Type
	  • Type of Dial-Up Server: (your selection automatically configures remote access protocol)
	Advanced options:
	  • Log on to network
	  • Enable software compression
	  • Require encrypted password
	Allowed network protocols:
	  • NetBEUI
	  • IPX/SPX Compatible
	  • TCP/IP
	  • TCPIP Settings

Connections	
Connect...	Makes connection using selected connection item in Dial-Up Networking folder.
Make New Connection...	Creates a new connection item.

Settings...	Lets you set Dial-Up Networking options:
	• Redial
	  • Before giving up retry
	  • Between tries wait
	• Prompt to use Dial-Up Networking
	• Don't prompt to use Dial-Up Networking

Direct Cable Connection

*Lets you connect to the local and network resources on a Windows 95
computer that is also running Direct Cable Connection.* **Direct Cable
Connection** *requires a null-modem serial or parallel cable.*

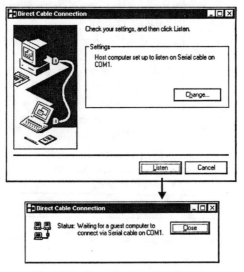

Direct Cable Connection from Host Computer

Location   Programs, Accessories

> *NOTE: If you did not install* **Direct Cable Connection**, *see*
> **Add or Remove Windows Components**, *page 91.*

Quick Start

1 Make sure the IPX/SPX-compatible protocol is installed (page 117)
   on both computers.
2 Connect a null-modem serial or parallel cable to the host and
   guest computers.

   NOTE: Be sure to use the same port type on each computer.

— FROM HOST COMPUTER —

3 Share folders the guest computer will access.
4 Configure computer as host, select the port and set a password
   (required if you are using User-level access control).
5 Click the Listen button.

— FROM GUEST COMPUTER —

6 Configure computer as guest and select the port.
7 Click the Connect button.

Direct Cable Connection (continued)

Direct Cable Connection Commands

Change	Lets you change settings for the computer:
	First dialog box:
	• Host — This computer has the resources you want to access.
	• Guest — This computer will be used to access resources on the host computer.
	Second dialog box:
	• Select the port you want to use
	• Install New Ports
	Third dialog box:
	• Use password protection
	• Set Password
Connect	Starts connection from guest computer.
Listen	Listens for guest connection on host computer.

Disk Defragmenter

*Moves **fragmented files** (files stored in non-consecutive pieces) so they are stored contiguously (in one piece) on a disk. This feature can improve disk performance.*

Select Drive ? X

Which drive do you want to defragment?

C on p5 (C:)

Copyright © 1985-1995 Microsoft Corporation
Copyright © 1988-1992 Symantec Corporation

OK   Exit

↓

Disk Defragmenter ? X

Drive C is 4 % fragmented.

You don't need to defragment this drive now. If you want to defragment it anyway, click Start.

Start   Select Drive   Advanced...   Exit

↓

Defragmenting Drive C _ □ X

0% Complete

Stop   Pause   Show Details

Disk Defragmenter Sequence

Location   Start   Programs, Accessories, System Tools

*NOTE: If you did not install **Disk Defragmenter**, see
Add or Remove Windows Components, page 91.*

What You Can Do with Disk Defragmenter

- Defragment any disk.
- Continue to work while Disk Defragmenter works.

Disk Defragmenter (continued)

Disk Defragmenter Commands

Start	Starts defragmenting the indicated drive.
Select Drive	Lets you selects a different drive. Disk Defragmenter automatically evaluates percentage of selected drive that is fragmented.

Advanced	Lets you set the following options:
	• Full defragmentation (both files and free space)
	• Defragment files only
	• Consolidate free space only
	• Check drive for errors
	• When do you want to use these options?
	   • This time only. Next time, use the defaults again.
	   • Save these options and use them every time.

Exit	Exits Disk Defragmenter program.

DriveSpace

Compresses files on a disk and provides commands to manage compressed disks.

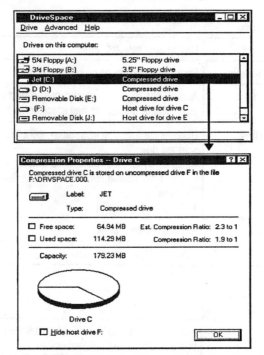

DriveSpace Showing Properties of a Compressed Drive

Location   📇Start   Programs, Accessories, System Tools

NOTE: If you did not install DriveSpace, see Add or Remove Windows Components, page 91.

Important Terms

- **Host drive** — An uncompressed drive that contains the Compressed Volume File (CVF).
- **Compressed Volume File (CVF)** — A hidden file stored on the host drive that contains all of the compressed files.
- **Mounting** — A DriveSpace action that assigns a drive letter to a Compressed Volume File, letting you use the files it contains. Mounting a drive normally occurs automatically when you start your computer.
- **Estimated compression ratio** — A ratio that determines the approximate space remaining on a compressed drive.

DriveSpace (continued)

Drive Space Menu Commands

Drive	
Compress...	Compresses selected drive.
Uncompress...	Removes compression on selected drive.
Adjust Free Space...	Adjusts free space on selected compressed drive by increasing or decreasing free space on its host drive.
Properties...	Displays the following information about the selected drive: • Label, Type, Free space, Used space, Est. Compression Ratio, Compression Ratio, Capacity • Hide host drive
Format...	Formats selected drive.
Exit	Exits DriveSpace program.

Advanced	
Mount...	Mounts compressed volume file on selected drive (makes compressed files accessible).
Unmount	Unmounts compressed volume file on selected drive (makes compressed files inaccessible).
Create Empty...	Creates new compressed drive from selected drive.
Delete...	Deletes selected drive.
Change Ratio...	Changes the estimated compression ratio on selected drive.
Change Letter...	Changes assigned letter of selected drive.
Settings...	Lets you set mounting options: • Automatically mount new compressed devices • (shows driver currently in use)
Refresh	Gets latest information about current drive.

HyperTerminal

*Lets you connect to a remote computer for the purpose of exchanging information and files. **HyperTerminal** requires a modem and an available phone connection.*

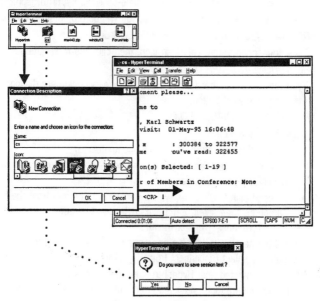

Making and Saving a Connection with HyperTerminal

Location 🏁 Start Programs, Accessories, HyperTerminal (folder)

NOTE: *If you did not install **HyperTerminal**, see Add or Remove Windows Components, page 91.*

What You Can Do with HyperTerminal

- Connect to another computer, even if that computer is not running Windows.
- Download (send) files to another computer.
- Upload (receive) files from another computer.
- Connect to computer bulletin boards.
- Connect to an online service, such as Compuserve.
- Send and receive email through an online service.
- Test your modem by entering modem commands, such as AT, in the HyperTerminal workspace area.

HyperTerminal (continued)

Quick Start

1   Open the HyperTerminal folder and double-click the Hypertrm icon.
    If you have not installed your modem, you will be prompted to do so.
— *FROM CONNECTION DESCRIPTION DIALOG BOX* —
2   Type connection name, select an icon, then click the **Next** button.
— *FROM PHONE NUMBER DIALOG BOX* —
3   Type the phone number for the computer or service you are dialing,
    then click the **Next** button.
— *FROM CONNECT DIALOG BOX* —
4   Click the **Dial** button.
5   Respond to the prompts from the host computer.

   • To change properties for the current session, select **Properties** from
      HyperTerminal's **File** menu.

   • To send or receive a file, wait for appropriate prompt from the host
      computer, then select **Send** File or **Receive** File from
      HyperTerminal's **Transfer** menu.

6   To end the session, select the appropriate command from the host
    computer or select **Disconnect** from HyperTerminal's **Call** menu.
7   When disconnected, exit HyperTerminal. Select **Yes** to save the
    connection information under the name and icon you selected above.

    Then, the next time you want to make the same connection, just
    double-click the icon you have saved. HyperTerminal stores saved
    session icons in the HyperTerminal folder.

HyperTerminal (continued)

HyperTerminal Menu Commands

File	
New Connection	Creates a new connection.
Open...	Opens a saved session file.
Save	Saves current session information using the current name.
Save As...	Saves and names current session information.
Page Setup...	Lets you set page options for printing.
Print...	Prints session data.
Properties	Lets you set properties for the current session. Phone Number properties include: • Change Icon • Country code • Area code • Phone number • Connect using (modem) • Configure *(See Set Modem Properties, page 175)* • Use country code and area code Settings properties include: Function, arrow, and ctrl keys act as • Terminal keys • Windows keys • Emulation • Terminal Setup • Backscroll buffer lines • Beep three times when connecting or disconnecting • ASCII Setup...

Continued ...

HyperTerminal (continued)

Edit	
Copy	Copies selected text in session to the Clipboard.
Paste to Host	Inserts text in the Clipboard into session workspace.
Select All	Selects all text in the session workspace.

View	
Tool Bar	Shows or hides the HyperTerminal toolbar.
Status Bar	Shows or hides the HyperTerminal status bar.
Font...	Lets you select a font.

Call	
Connect	Starts a new connection.
Disconnect	Ends current connection.

Transfer	
Send File...	Lets you select a file to send, a protocol for the transfer, and begins the send process.
Receive File...	Lets you select a folder in which to receive a file, a protocol for the transfer, and begins the receive process.
Capture Text...	Lets you capture session text to a text file.
Send Text File...	Lets you send a text file to the host computer.
Capture to Printer	Sends session information to the printer as it occurs.

Media Player

Plays multimedia files, such as video files and compact discs. To take advantage of Media Player you should have an installed sound card.

```
🎛 Jungle Menu Popup.wav - Media Player (sto...  _ □ ✕
File  Edit  Device  Scale  Help
```

Media Player

Location 🏁 Start Programs, Accessories, Multimedia

> *NOTE: If you did not install **Media Player**, see **Add or Remove Windows Components**, page 91.*

What You Can Do with Media Player

- Play video (.AVI) files.
- Play sound (.WAV) files.
- Play MIDI sequencer (.MID and .RMI) files.
- Play CD compact discs.
- Play multimedia files within a document.
- Play multimedia files by double-clicking them.
- Set properties of selected multimedia device.
- Copy a multimedia file (or parts of it) into a document.
- Link a multimedia file to one or more documents.

Media Player Controls

The illustration below identifies Media Player's controls.

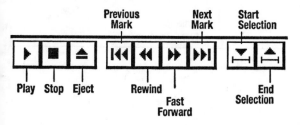

Media Player (continued)

Media Player Menu Commands

File	
Open...	Lets you open a multimedia file.
Close	Closes open multimedia file.
Exit	Closes Media Player.

Edit	
Copy Object	Copies the open multimedia file to the Clipboard as an object. You can then paste the object into an OLE application (such as WordPad). You can play the file by double-clicking it. *NOTE: You can copy part of the file (see Selection, below) and you can set options for the object (see Options, below.).*
Options	Lets you select the following file options: • Auto Rewind • Auto Repeat OLE Object • Control Bar On Playback • Caption • Border around object • Play in client document • Dither picture to VGA colors
Selection...	Lets you select the following file parts: • All • None • From, To, Size

Continued ...

Media Player (continued)

Device	
1 Video for Windows...	Lets you open a multimedia file type.
2 Sound...	*(Device option may vary.)*
3 MIDI Sequencer...	
4 CD Audio	Plays an audio compact disc.
Properties	Lets you view or change properties for the device associated with the open multimedia file.
Volume Control	Opens the Volume Control from which you can set volume options.

Scale	
Time	Selects a scale for the open file.
Frame	
Tracks	

Microsoft Backup

Backs up files to a local, network or tape drive. You can then use Backup to restore or compare backed up files.

Microsoft Backup with Open File Set

Location   [Start]   Programs, Accessories, System Tools

> *NOTE: If you did not install **Microsoft Backup**, see
> **Add or Remove Windows Components**, page 91.*

Important Terms

- File set — A file containing a list of folders and files to back up and the backup destination.
  TIP: You can double-click a file set icon to perform a backup quickly.
- Backup set — A file stored on a drive or tape that contains the files you have backed up.

Quick Start

1. From the Backup tab, select files and folders to back up, or open a file set (File, Open File Set) and click **Next Step >** button.
2. Select destination for the backup (drive, folder or tape drive).
3. If desired, save your backup settings (File, Save As).
4. Click Start Backup.

Microsoft Backup (continued)

Microsoft Backup Menu Commands

File	
Open File Set...	Lets you open a file set.
Close	Closes current file set and/or removes all folder and file selections.
Save	Saves opened file set using current selections.
Save As...	Lets you save and name a new file set using current selections.
Page Setup...	Lets you set paper size, source, orientation and margins for printing.
Print...	Prints information about current file set.
Refresh	Gets latest information about drives and folders.
Exit	Exits Microsoft Backup program.

Settings	
File Filtering...	Lets you exclude files to back up by date modified or file type.
Drag and Drop...	Lets you set how Backup will run when you launch it by dragging a file set icon onto the Backup icon.
	Drag and Drop options include: • Run Backup minimized • Confirm operation before beginning • Quit Backup after operation is finished

Continued ...

Microsoft Backup (continued)

Settings	*continued*

Options...	Lets you set Microsoft Backup options.
	
	General options include:
	• Turn on audible prompts
	• Overwrite old status log files
	
	Backup options include:
	• Quit Backup after operation is finished
	Type of backup
	  • Full
	  • Incremental: backup of selected files that have changed since last full backup
	Advanced options
	  • Verify backup data by automatically comparing files after backup is finished
	  • Use data compression
	  • Format when needed on tape backups
	  • Always erase on tape backups
	  • Always erase on floppy disk backups
	
	Restore options include:
	• Quit Backup after operation is finished
	Restore backed up files to
	  • Original locations
	  • Alternate location
	  • Alternate location, single directory
	Advanced options
	  • Verify restored data by automatically comparing files after the restore has finished
	  • Never overwrite files
	  • Overwrite older files only
	  • Overwrite files
	  • Prompt before overwriting files
	
	Compare options include:
	• Quit Backup after operation is finished
	Location of Compare
	  • Original locations
	  • Alternate location
	  • Alternate location, single directory

Continued ...

Microsoft Backup (continued)

Tools	
Format Tape...	Prepares a tape for use by Backup.
Erase Tape...	Deletes all data on tape in tape drive.
Redetect Tape Drive...	Detects if tape drive is installed.

Microsoft Backup Tab Procedures

Backup	
left pane	Lets you select folders to back up.
right pane	Lets you select folders or files to back up.
Next Step >	Starts the next step in the backup process.

Restore	
left pane	Lets you open folder containing backup set.
right pane	Lets you select backup set to restore.
Next Step >	Starts the next step in the restore process.
left pane	Lets you select folders from back up set to restore.
right pane	Lets you select files from backup set to restore.
Start Restore	Begins restore process.

Compare	
left pane	Lets you open folder containing backup set.
right pane	Lets you select backup set to compare.
Next Step >	Starts the next step in the compare process.
left pane	Lets you select folders to compare.
right pane	Lets you select or deselect files to compare.
Start Compare	Starts compare process.

Microsoft Exchange

Lets you send, receive and manage electronic messages and faxes from one location.

Microsoft Exchange Viewer

Location   [🏁 Start] Programs

> *NOTE: If you did not install **Microsoft Exchange**, see*
> ***Add or Remove Windows Components**, page 91.*

What You Can Do with Microsoft Exchange

- Send and retrieve messages using many network and online information services such as: Microsoft Mail, Microsoft Fax, Internet Mail, The Microsoft Network, and CompuServe R Mail Services.

- Send messages with varied content:
  - rich-text documents as faxes
  - include files and OLE objects

- Manage your messages in one place. For example, you can sort the messages you have received from Microsoft Mail and CompuServe. Then, you can sort the messages by priority, or filter them to see only messages from a specific user.

- Create folders in which to store related messages.

- Set up profiles from which you can choose when you start Microsoft Exchange. One profile might be set up to dial into an online information service and retrieve mail, while another profile might be set up to exchange mail and faxes on a local area network.

Microsoft Exchange (continued)

Important Terms

- **Workgroup postoffice** — A special structure of folders that stores Mail items such as messages and postoffice users information. When you install Microsoft Exchange, you will have to indicate the location and name of the postoffice (i.e., C:\windows\wgpo0000) or create it. On a network, the postoffice is shared with other users.

- **Information service** — Messaging systems from which Microsoft Exchange can receive or send information.

- **Personal Address Book (PAB)** — Stores your email addresses, names, phone numbers, fax numbers, and contact information. The Personal address book is accessible through other applications.

- **Personal Information Store (PST)** — A storage system for your messages, forms and documents containing the following folders:

    Inbox — A folder that receives new messages when you connect to information services such as Microsoft Mail or the Internet.

    Outbox — A folder that stores messages you are sending.

    Sent items — A folder that stores copies of sent items.

    Deleted Items — A folder that stores deleted messages.

- **Profile** — Stores information about the information services you have added and settings for how mail is delivered. You can set up more than one profile.

Microsoft Exchange Viewer Toolbar

The illustration below identifies the default buttons on the Microsoft Exchange Viewer toolbar.

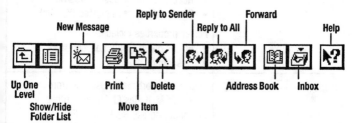

Microsoft Exchange (continued)

Microsoft Exchange Viewer Menu Commands

File	
Open	Lets you open selected message.
Save As...	Lets you save selected message in one of the following file formats: Text Only, Rich Text Format, Message Format
Move...	Moves selected message(s) to another folder in Personal Information Store.
Copy...	Copies selected message(s) to another folder in Personal Information Store.
Print...	Prints selected message(s).
New Folder...	Creates new folder below selected folder in folder pane.
Delete	Deletes selected folder or message(s).
Rename...	Renames selected folder.
Properties	Lets you view or change properties of selected message or folder. **Message properties include:** • Message subject, Type, Size, Location • Sent, Received, Last changed • Importance — High, Normal, Low • Sensitivity • Read Receipt requested (Yes/No) • Delivery Receipt requested (Yes/No) **Folder properties include:** • Folder name, Type, Location • Description
Import...	Lets you import mail messages from Microsoft Mail files (.MMF) and other Personal Address Book files (.PAB).
Exit	Exits Microsoft Exchange program.
Exit and Log Off	Exits Microsoft Exchange program and logs you off.

Continued ...

Microsoft Exchange (continued)

Edit	
Select All	Selects all messages in the current folder.
Mark as Read	Marks selected message as read (unbolded).
Mark as Unread	Marks selected message as unread (bolded).

View	
Folders	Shows or hides folders in Personal Information Store.
Toolbar	Shows or hides toolbar.
Status Bar	Shows or hides status bar.
New Window	Opens a duplicate window for Personal Information Store.
Columns...	Lets you add columns to or remove columns from the message area.
Group By...	Lets you group and sort message items.
Sort...	Lets you sort message items.

Continued ...

Microsoft Exchange (continued)

Tools	NOTE: Your options may differ.
Deliver Now/ Deliver Now Using	Sends selected message(s) using current or selected information service.
Address Book	Opens address book.
Find...	Finds messages containing the criteria you specify such as: subject, message body, and advanced criteria, such as a date range.
Remote Mail	Opens message window from which you can connect to a remote information service to collect and transfer email.
Customize Toolbar...	Lets you add to or remove buttons from the toolbar.

Microsoft Fax Tools	Lets you set the following options:
	• Request a Fax
	• Advanced Security
	• Show Outgoing Faxes
	• Options (properties)
	   Message
	   Dialing
	   Modem
	   User

Microsoft Mail Tools	Lets you set the following options: • Change Mailbox Password • Download Address Lists • Schedule Remote Mail Delivery • View Session Log
Services...	Lets you add or remove information services to the current profile.

Continued ...

Microsoft Exchange (continued)

Tools	continued
Options...	Lets you set Microsoft Exchange properties. General properties include: • When new mail arrives... • Deleting items... • When starting Microsoft Exchange... • Show ToolTips on toolbars • When selecting, automatically select entire word Read properties include: • After moving or deleting an open item... • When replying to or forwarding an item... • Use this font for the reply text: Font Send properties include: When sending mail... • Use this font: Font • Request that a receipt be sent back when... • Set sensitivity • Set importance: High, Normal, Low • Save a copy of the item in the Sent Items folder Spelling properties include: • Always suggest replacements for misspelled words • Always check spelling before sending • When checking, always ignore... Services properties include: • Add or Remove information services and set Properties for an information service. Delivery properties include: • Deliver new mail to the following location • Secondary location • Recipient addresses are processed by these information services in the following order Addressing properties include: • Show this address list first • Keep personal addresses in • When sending mail, check names using these address lists in the following order • Add, Remove or set Properties of address lists.

Continued ...

Microsoft Exchange (continued)

Compose	NOTE: Your options may differ.
New Message	Opens message window from which you can: • Address the message. • Type the subject and text. • Set importance indicator. • Insert a file. • Send the message.
New Fax	Opens Compose New Fax dialog box from which you can: • Address the fax. • Select cover page options. • Set fax options such as: Time the fax is sent, message format, Dialing, Security... • Type subject and note. • Add files. • Send the fax.
Reply to Sender	Opens message window from which you can reply to the sender of selected message.
Reply to All	Opens message window from which you can reply to all messages from sender of selected message.
Forward	Opens message window from which you can forward selected message(s) to other users.

Microsoft Fax

A service you add to Microsoft Exchange that lets you compose, address and send fax messages.

Compose New Fax

To: [   ] [Address Book..]

Country: [United States of America (1)   ▼]

Fax #: ([718]) [980-0909]   ☐ Dial area code

⇩ [Add to List]

Recipient list:

Kathy B (Fax)

[Remove]

[< Back] [Next >] [Cancel]

Compose New Fax Wizard

Location   🏁 Start   Programs, Accessories, Fax

NOTE: *The location above is for the Compose New Fax application and other fax utilities. You can send a fax message in other ways as described below. If you did not install **Microsoft Fax**, see **Add or Remove Windows Components**, page 91.*

What You Can Do with Microsoft Fax

- Compose or send a fax document in the following ways:
  - From Microsoft Exchange — Compose, address and attach a file to a fax.
  - From a Windows application — By printing to the Microsoft Fax printer.
  - From any Windows folder — By dragging a document onto a shortcut to the Microsoft Fax printer icon.
  - From any MAPI-enabled application (such as Microsoft Word) — By selecting Send from the File menu.
- Attach editable documents to faxes that can be opened by a recipient who is also using Microsoft Fax. If the recipient is a fax machine, Microsoft Fax automatically renders the file as an image.

Continued ...

Microsoft Fax (continued)

- Set security options to ensure only the intended recipient can read the fax message.
- Share a fax modem with others on a network and control its use with a password.
- Manage queued faxes with Fax Queue Viewer.
- Connect to fax information services to retrieve faxes.
- Use the Microsoft Exchange inbox and address book system to retrieve and manage fax messages.
- Send fax messages to recipients in different information services simultaneously.

Fax Utilities

When you install Microsoft Fax, Windows installs the utilities below to help you compose and work with fax messages.

Utility	Location and description:
Compose New Fax	Programs, Accessories, Fax Compose New Fax lets you compose, address and send a fax.
Cover Page Editor	Programs, Accessories, Fax Cover Page Editor lets you edit or create fax cover pages.
Fax Viewer	Opens automatically when you double-click an attached fax icon in a message. Fax messages are stored in the Microsoft Exchange inbox. Fax Viewer lets you view and format rendered faxes you have received.
Request a Fax	Programs, Accessories, Fax Lets you connect to fax information services to retrieve faxes.

Microsoft Fax (continued)

Compose New Fax Wizard Commands

The following tables describe the Compose New Fax Wizard commands for each dialog box (step).

Step 1	NOTE: This step can be disabled.
I'm dialing from	Shows where you are dialing from.
Dialing Properties	Lets you set dialing properties: Where I am: • I am dialing from (location) • New, Remove (location) • The area code is • I am in (country) How I dial from this location: • To access an outside line, first dial *n* for local and *n* for long distance • Dial using Calling Card • This location has call waiting. To disable it, dial *n*. The phone system at this location uses: • Tone dialing, Pulse dialing
I'm not using a portable computer, so ...	Disables this step when sending next fax.
Next >	Starts the next step in fax process.

Step 2	
To	Receives recipient's name.
Address Book	Lets you select recipient from an address book.
Country	Lets you select country of recipient.
Fax #	Receives recipient's fax number.
Dial area code	Dials area code if selected.
Add to List	Adds recipient to Recipient list.
Remove	Removes selected recipient in Recipient list.
Next >	Starts the next step in fax process.

Continued ...

Microsoft Fax (continued)

Step 3	
Do you want a cover page? **N<u>o</u>** **<u>Y</u>es**	Selects cover page option. If you select <u>Y</u>es, select cover page type in list.

<u>O</u>ptions	Lets you set fax options:
	 Time to send
	 • As s<u>o</u>on as possible
	 • Dis<u>c</u>ount rates
	 • Spe<u>c</u>ific time
	 • <u>S</u>et (specific time)
	 Message format
	 • <u>E</u>ditable, if possible
	 • <u>E</u>ditable only
	 • <u>N</u>ot editable
	 • <u>P</u>aper
	    <u>P</u>aper size
	    <u>I</u>mage quality
	    Orientation (P<u>o</u>rtrait/<u>L</u>andscape)
	 Cover page
	 • Send co<u>v</u>er page
	 • <u>B</u>rowse
	 • <u>D</u>ialing
	    • <u>D</u>ialing Properties
	    • T<u>o</u>ll Prefixes
	    • <u>N</u>umber of retries
	    • <u>T</u>imes between retries
	 • <u>S</u>ecurity method
	    • <u>N</u>one
	    • <u>K</u>ey-encrypted
	    • <u>P</u>assword-protected
	    • <u>D</u>igitally sign all attachments

Next >	Starts the next step in fax process.

Continued ...

Microsoft Fax (continued)

Step 4	
Subject	Receives subject of fax.
Note	Receives fax note text.
Start note on cover page	Sets fax to print note on cover page.
Next >	Starts the next step in fax process.

Step 5	
Files to send	Lists files you have added to fax.
Add File	Lets you select a file to attach to the fax.
Remove	Removes selected file from fax.
Next >	Starts the next step in fax process.

Step 6	
Finish	Sends the fax.

Net Watcher

Lets you monitor, manage and create network shares on your computer and administer network shares on a remote computer.

Shared Folder	Shared As	Access Type	Comment
C:\	C	User Depen...	
C:\NETFAX	FAX	User Depen...	Network fax server
C:\WIN95\PROFILE...	WIN JOB	User Depen...	
C:\WIN95\WGPO00...	WGPO0000	User Depen...	Postoffice for MS Mail
D:\	D	User Depen...	D drive on P5win95
D:\WP\CHICAGO\A...	ART	User Depen...	D:\wp\chicago\art
E:\	E	User Depen...	CDROM on P5win95

Net Watcher Window

Location   ▓Start Programs, Accessories, System Tools

*NOTE: If you did not install **Net Watcher**, see **Add or Remove Windows Components**, page 91.*

What You Can Do with Net Watcher

- Show connections made to shared folders on your computer.
- Show files opened by others on your computer.
- Administer a remote computer:
  - Add and delete shares.
  - Monitor connections and files opened.

Required Services and Security Notes

- Net Watcher requires File and Printer Sharing services on your computer and the remote computers.
- If you are using share-level security, you can only use Net Watcher to connect to other computers using share-level security.
- If you are using user-level security, you can use Net Watcher to connect to other computers using share-level or user-level security.

Net Watcher (continued)

Net Watcher Toolbar

The illustration below identifies the buttons on Net Watchers toolbar.

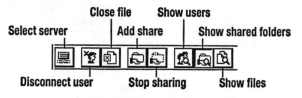

Net Watcher Menu Commands

Administer	
Select Server...	Lets you select server to administer. (Requires that Remote Administration is enabled on the remote computer.)
Disconnect User	Disconnects selected user. (Requires the by Connection view.)
Close File	Closes selected file. (Requires the by Open Files view.)
Add Shared Folder...	Lets you add a folder to share with others. (Requires the by Shared Folders view.)
Stop Sharing Folder	Stops sharing selected folder with others. (Requires the by Shared Folders view.)
Shared Folder Properties...	Lets you change share properties for selected folder. (Requires the by Shared Folders view.)

Continued ...

Net Watcher (continued)

View	
by <u>C</u>onnection	Shows connections to this server in left pane. Shows shared folders connected to (and files opened in) right pane.
by <u>S</u>hared Folders	Shows shared folders and printers in left pane. Shows connections to selected share (and files opened) in right pane.
by <u>O</u>pen Files	Shows files opened by other users.
<u>T</u>oolbar	Shows or hides Net Watcher toolbar.
Status <u>B</u>ar	Shows or hides Net Watcher status bar.
Lar<u>g</u>e Icons **S<u>m</u>all Icons** **<u>D</u>etails**	Lets you select appearance of items in Net Watcher.
<u>R</u>efresh	Obtains latest information about connections.

Notepad

Lets you create and edit text files.

```
┌──────────────────────────────────────────────┐
│ ▤ Untitled - Notepad                  _ □ ✕   │
│ File  Edit  Search  Help                       │
│ ┌────────────────────────────────────────┐ ▲ │
│ │                                        │   │
│ │                                        │   │
│ │                                        │   │
│ │                                        │   │
│ │                                        │   │
│ │                                        │   │
│ │                                        │   │
│ │                                        │ ▼ │
│ ◄                                       ► │   │
└──────────────────────────────────────────────┘
```

Notepad Window

Location   Programs, Accessories

> *NOTE: If you did not install **Notepad**, see **Add or Remove Windows Components**, page 91.*

What You Can Do with Notepad

- Create and edit ASCII text files.*
- Cut, copy and paste text to and from the Clipboard.
- Search for specified text.
- Insert the system time and date into a document.
- Set word wrap on or off.
- Apply page format commands, including margins, headers and footers.
- Print documents.

NOTE: Files created with Notepad are in ASCII format. ASCII text contains plain, unformatted text. Notepad is especially useful for editing batch (.BAT) files and Windows (.INI) files.

Notepad (continued)

Notepad Menu Commands

File	
New	Starts a new, untitled document.
Open...	Lets you open a document stored on disk.
Save	Saves document.
Save **A**s...	Lets you save and rename current document.
Page Se**t**up...	Lets you set print options, such as paper size, source, orientation, margins, header, footer and select a printer.
Print	Prints current document.
E**x**it	Exits the Notepad program.

Edit	
Undo	Restores previous deletion.
Cu**t**	Removes selected text and places it in the Clipboard.
Copy	Copies selected text to the Clipboard.
Paste	Inserts text in Clipboard into current document.
De**l**ete	Deletes selected text.
Select **A**ll	Selects all text in current document.
Time/**D**ate	Inserts time and date into current document.
Word Wrap	Enables or disables word wrap.

Search	
Find...	Lets you search document for specified text.
Find **N**ext	Continues search using previous search criteria.

Paint

Lets you create and edit bitmap drawings.

Paint Window

Location   [Start] Programs, Accessories

> *NOTE: If you did not install **Paint**, see **Add or Remove Windows Components**, page 91.*

What You Can Do with Paint

- Create and edit bitmap graphics with text.
- Cut, copy and paste sections of drawings to the Clipboard or a file.
- Select a variety of fonts and font sizes when using text.
- Magnify drawings for detailed editing.
- Preview and print drawings.
- Link or embed objects (drawings or parts of drawings) into other applications.
- Set current drawing as a wallpaper pattern.

Paint (continued)

Paint Menu Commands

File	
New	Closes open file and starts a new, untitled file.
Open...	Lets you open a file stored on disk.
Save	Saves current file.
Save As...	Lets you save and name current file.
Print Preview	Previews current file as it would be printed.
Page Setup...	Lets you set print options, such as paper size, source, orientation, margins and select a printer.
Print...	Prints current file.
Send...	Lets you send the current file as a message. (Requires Microsoft Exchange.)
Set As Wallpaper (Tiled)	Sets current file as wallpaper on your desktop and repeats the graphic in a side-by-side arrangement.
Set As Wallpaper (Centered)	Sets current file as wallpaper on your desktop and centers it.
Exit	Exits the Paint program.

Edit	
Undo	Reverses your last action.
Repeat	Repeats your last action.
Cut	Removes selected area of drawing to Clipboard.
Copy	Copies selected area of drawing to Clipboard.
Paste	Inserts data in the Clipboard into current file.
Clear Selection	Deletes selected area of drawing.
Select All	Selects entire drawing workspace.
Copy To...	Lets you copy selected area of drawing to a file stored on disk.
Paste From...	Inserts data stored in a file into current file.

Continued ...

Paint (continued)

View	
Tool Box	Shows or hides the tool box.
Color Box	Shows or hides the color box.
Status Bar	Shows or hides the status bar.
Zoom ▶	Lets you select one of the following magnifications: Normal Size Large Size Custom... Show Grid Show Thumbnail
View Bitmap...	Fills screen with drawing.
Text Toolbar	Shows or hides text toolbar when using text tool.

Image	
Flip/Rotate...	Lets you flip or rotate selection or entire drawing: • Flip horizontal • Flip vertical • Rotate by angle — 90°, 180°, 270°
Stretch/Skew...	Lets you stretch or skew selection or entire drawing: Stretch • Horizontal (%) • Vertical (%) Skew • Horizontal (degrees) • Vertical (degrees)
Invert Colors	Inverts colors for selection or entire drawing.

Attributes...	Lets you change attributes of the current drawing:
	• Width
	• Height
	  Units
	  • Inches, Cm, Pels
	  Colors
	  • Black and white, Colors
	• Default

Clear Image	Clears entire drawing.

Continued ...

Paint (continued)

Options	
E̲dit Colors...	Lets you create a custom color for selected color in the color box.
G̲et Colors...	Replaces current color box with saved color palette.
S̲ave Colors...	Saves current color box as a saved color palette on disk.
D̲raw Opaque	Enables or disables opaque Draw mode. This effects what shows through after moving a selection on another part of the drawing. **When disabled:** Destination area of drawing shows through selected drawing and background of selection is not used. **When enabled:** Background and foreground of selection covers destination area of drawing.

Paint Color Palette

The illustration below shows how to select the foreground and background colors from the Color Palette.

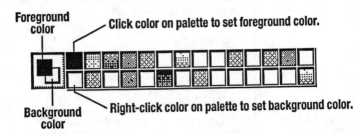

Paint (continued)

Paint Tool Box
The illustration below identifies the buttons on Paint's tool box.

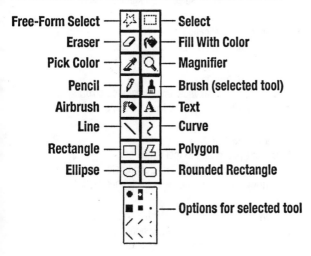

Free-Form Select — Select
Eraser — Fill With Color
Pick Color — Magnifier
Pencil — Brush (selected tool)
Airbrush — Text
Line — Curve
Rectangle — Polygon
Ellipse — Rounded Rectangle

— Options for selected tool

Free-Form Select — Selects free-form part of drawing.
Drag to draw a free-form shape around area to select.
Drag area within dotted rectangle to move selection.
Drag handles on rectangle to size the selection.
You can cut, copy or clear selection. (Options are on Edit menu.)

Select — Selects rectangular part of drawing.
Drag to draw rectangle around area to select.
Drag area within dotted rectangle to move selection.
Handles indicate areas to drag to size the selection.
You can cut, copy or clear selection. (Options are on Edit menu).

Eraser — Erases part of drawing.
Select eraser size in tool option box.
Drag eraser through drawing to erase.

Fill With Color — Fills enclosed part of drawing.
Click in a closed shape to fill it with foreground color.
Right-click in a closed shape to fill it with background color.

Continued ..

Paint (continued)

Pick Color — Selects a color from drawing.
    Click color in drawing to select a foreground color.
    Right-click color in drawing to select a background color.

Magnifier — Changes magnification.
    Click desired magnification (1x, 2x, 6x, 8x) in tool option box.

Pencil — Draws a free-form line.
    Drag to draw a line one pixel wide with foreground color.
    Right-drag to draw a line one pixel wide with background color.

Brush — Draws a free-form line.
    Select a brush size and shape in tool option box.
    Drag to draw a free-form line with foreground color.
    Right-drag to draw a free-form line with background color.

Airbrush — Draws with selected airbrush size and shape.
    Select an airbrush size and shape in tool option box.
    Drag to draw a free-form pattern with foreground color.
    Right-drag to draw a free-form pattern with background color.

Text — Inserts text in drawing.
    Drag through drawing to create a text frame where text can be typed.
    If necessary, show the text toolbar (View, Text Toolbar).
    Select font and font attribute(s) on text toolbar.
    Click inside the text frame and type the text.
    Click desired background option (enabled or disabled) in tool option box.
    Right-click the desired background color if background color is enabled.
    Click a color in the color palette to change the text color.
    Drag the text frame to move or enlarge it.

Line — Draws a straight line.
    Select line width in tool option box.
    Click desired color for line in color palette.
    Drag a line to draw with foreground color.
    Right-drag a line to draw with background color.

Continued ...

Paint (continued)

Curve — Draws a curved line.
    Select line width in tool option box.
    Click desired color for line in color palette.
    Drag a straight line, then click a point on that line to mark curve point
        and drag the curve point to make an arc.

Rectangle and Rounded Rectangle — Draws a rectangle.
    Select rectangle style in tool option box.
    Click desired color for line in color palette.
    Right-click color in color palette to select a fill color.
    Drag through drawing to draw the rectangle.

Polygon — Draws a polygon.
    Select polygon style in tool option box.
    Click desired color for line in color palette.
    Right-click color in color palette to select a fill color.
    Drag through drawing and click to create each corner, then double-click
        to complete the shape.

Ellipse — Draws a rounded rectangle.
    Select ellipse style in tool option box.
    Click desired color for line in color palette.
    Right-click color in color palette to select a fill color.
    Drag through drawing to draw the ellipse.

Phone Dialer

Lets you record and dial phone numbers from your computer. To use Phone Dialer you need a modem and an available phone line.

Phone Dialer

Location   🏁 Start   Programs, Accessories

> *NOTE: If you did not install **Phone Dialer**, see **Add or Remove Windows Components**, page 91.*

What You Can Do with Phone Dialer

- Store frequently used numbers in a speed-dial list.
- Dial phone numbers by clicking a speed-dial button.
- Dial phone numbers by typing the number and clicking Dial.
- Dial phone numbers by clicking the number buttons and clicking Dial.
- Keep a log of outgoing and incoming phone calls. The phone log includes the person, phone number, date, time and length of call.
- Call numbers directly from the phone log.

Phone Dialer (continued)

Phone Dialer Menu Commands

File	
E**x**it	Exits Phone Dialer program.

Edit	
Cu**t**	Removes selected text and places it in the Clipboard.
Copy	Copies selected text to the Clipboard.
Paste	Inserts text in Clipboard into current document.
Delete	Deletes selected text.
Speed Dial...	Lets you assign names and phone numbers to speed-dial buttons: 1 Click the button to assign. 2 Type the name in the **N**ame box. 3 Type the phone number in the N**u**mber to dial box. 4 Repeat steps above for each number to assign. 5 Click **S**ave when done.

Continued ...

Phone Dialer (continued)

Tools	
Connect Using...	Lets you set the following options: • Line (Select phone line or modem for dialing.) • Line Properties (Sets modem properties *(see page 175).*) • Address (Select phone number for dialing out.) • Use Phone Dialer to handle voice call requests from other programs
Dialing Properties...	Lets you set dialing properties: Where I am: • I am dialing from (location) • New, Remove (location) • The area code is • I am in (country) How I dial from this location: • To access an outside line, first dial *n* for local and *n* for long distance. • Dial using Calling Card • This location has call waiting. To disable it, dial *n*. The phone system at this location uses • Tone dialing, Pulse dialing • Dial as a long distance call
Show Log	Opens a Call Log window from which you can: • Specify the types of calls (incoming or outgoing) to log (Log, Options). • Dial number of selected item in log (Log, Dial) • Cut, copy and delete selected log items (from Edit menu).

ScanDisk

Scans and fixes errors found on disks.

ScanDisk Window

Location	[Start] Programs, Accessories, System Tools

NOTE. If you did not install **ScanDisk,** *see* **Add or Remove Windows Components,** *page 91.*

What You Can Do with ScanDisk

- Check and fix errors found in your files and folders.
- Check and fix errors found on the surface of your disks.
- Run ScanDisk each time you start your computer.
  To do this:
  - Create shortcut (page 88) for SCANDSKW.EXE to the StartUp folder.
  - Right-click the shortcut and select Properties
  - Click the Shortcut tab and add parameters to the command in the Target text box as in these examples:
    SCANDSKW.EXE /a /n /p   SCANDSKW.EXE c: /n
    Meaning of switches:
    - /a   check and repair all drives (you can specify a drive instead).
    - /n   sets ScanDisk to close automatically when done.
    - /p   prevent ScanDisk from fixing errors it finds.

ScanDisk (continued)

ScanDisk Commands

Type of test	
Standard	Sets test to check files and folders for errors.
Thorough	Sets test to check files and folders for errors and scans disk surface for errors.
Options...	Lets you set the following surface scan options: Areas of disk to scan • System and data areas. • System area only. • Data area only. • Do not perform write-testing. • Do not repair bad sectors in hidden and system files.
Automatically fix errors	Sets ScanDisk to fix errors without prompting you.
Advanced...	Lets you set ScanDisk advanced options: Display summary • Always, Never, Only if errors found Log file • Replace log, Append to log, No log Cross-linked files • Delete, Make copies, Ignore Lost file fragments • Free, Convert to files Check files for • Invalid file names, Invalid dates and times • Check host drive first
Start	Begins ScanDisk process.

Sound Recorder

Lets you record, play back and edit sounds. To use Sound Recorder you need a sound card and a microphone if you want to record sounds.

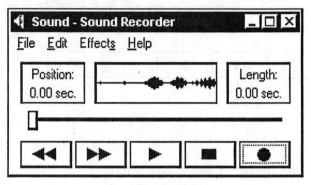

Sound Recorder Window

Location   Programs, Accessories, Multimedia

> *NOTE: If you did not install **Sound Recorder**, see*
> ***Add or Remove Windows Components**, page 91.*

What You Can Do with Sound Recorder

- Play sound files.
- Record and edit sound files that you can then assign to system events.
- Modify sounds by inserting or mixing other sound files.
- Modify sounds by inserting or mixing sounds copied to the Clipboard.
- Add echo effects and increase or decrease volume and playback speed.
- Reverse sounds.
- Link or embed sound files (objects) into other applications.

Sound Recorder (continued)

Sound Recorder Controls

The illustration below identifies the Sound Recorder controls.

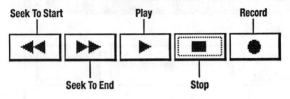

Seek To Start   **Play**   **Record**

Seek To End   **Stop**

Sound Recorder Menu Commands

File	
New	Starts a new, untitled file.
Open...	Lets you open a sound file stored on disk.
Save	Saves current sound file.
Save As...	Lets you save and rename current sound file.
Revert...	Reverts current sound file to its last saved state.
Properties	Let you view or set the following properties for the current sound: • Sound file name, Copyright, Length, Data Size, Audio Format Format Conversion • Choose from (select a format) • Convert Now
Exit	Exits Sound Recorder program.

Continued ...

Sound Recorder (continued)

Edit	
Copy	Copies current sound to the Clipboard.
Paste Insert	Inserts sound in Clipboard into current sound.
Paste Mix	Mixes sound in Clipboard with current sound at slider position.
Insert File...	Lets you select a file to insert into current sound as slider position.
Mix with File...	Lets you select a sound file to mix with current sound file at slider position.
Delete Before Current Position	Deletes all of the current sound that exists before the slider position.
Delete After Current Position	Deletes all of the current sound that exists after the slider position.
Audio Properties	Lets you set audio properties: Playback • Volume • Preferred device • Show volume control on the taskbar Recording • Volume • Preferred device • Preferred quality • Customize • Use preferred devices only

Continued ...

Sound Recorder (continued)

Effects	
Increase Volume (by 25%)	Increases sound speed by 25%.
Decrease Volume	Decreases sound volume.
Increase Speed (by 100%)	Increases sound speed by 100%
Decrease Speed	Decreases sound speed.
Add Echo	Adds echo effect to sound.
Reverse	Reverses the sound.

The Microsoft Network

Lets you access the MSN (The Microsoft Network) — an online information service. The Microsoft Network requires a modem and a phone line.

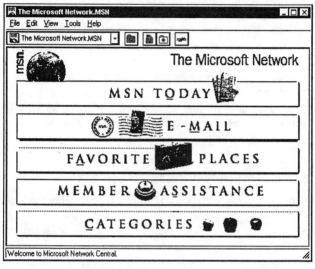

MSN Central

Location 　🏁Start　 Programs

> *NOTE: If you did not install **The Microsoft Network**, see **Add or Remove Windows Components**, page 91.*

What You Can Do with the Microsoft Network

- Send and receive information:
  - Exchange messages (email) with other members.
  - Converse with MSN members in a chat room.
  - Exchange information and mail with MSN members from other parts of the world using (in most cases) a local phone call.
  - Post and respond to messages in one of many bulletin boards (BBS) set up on a variety of topics.
  - From file libraries, download program updates, game software, graphics and articles.
  - Connect to various information services to read about news, sports, gardening, science and other topics.
  - Obtain technical support from Microsoft and other service providers.

Continued ...

The Microsoft Network (continued)

- Take advantage of the common Windows 95 interface:
  - You can drag and drop items to copy them.
  - You can navigate folder windows by double-clicking folders or using the toolbar as you do when navigating local folders.
  - You can create shortcuts to a favorite place by right-clicking it, and selecting Add to Favorite Places.
  - You can use Windows Explorer to navigate the contents of the Microsoft Network.
- Take advantage of Windows 95 multi-tasking which allows you to perform other activities within Microsoft Network while a file is downloading, for example.

The Microsoft Network Central Options

MSN TODAY	Keeps you up-to-date on new services and special events.
E-MAIL	Starts Microsoft Exchange, from which you can send mail to and receive it from other members.
FAVORITE PLACES	A folder that stores icons you can open to access your favorite services.
MEMBER ASSISTANCE	Contains Help for the Microsoft Network and other member-related services.
CATEGORIES	Contains the forums and topics that make up MSN. A forum may include chat rooms, bulletin boards (BBS), file libraries, and a Kiosk. Kiosks provide details about new additions, the forum manager and other information specific to the forum.

The Microsoft Network Toolbar

The illustration below identifies the buttons on the MSN toolbar when in the Favorite Places, Member Assistance and Categories folder windows.

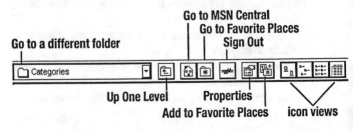

The Microsoft Network (continued)

The Microsoft Network Menu Commands

The commands that follow are contained in the Favorite Places, Member Assistance and Categories folder windows.

NOTE: MSN folders also contain menus common to all folders in Windows. Those menu items are not covered here.

File	
Open	Opens selected item.
Explore	Opens an Explorer view showing a hierarchy of folders in the Microsoft Network.
Delete	Deletes selected item in Favorite Places.
Create Shortcut	Creates a shortcut for the selected item and places it on your desktop. You can then double-click the shortcut to start the Microsoft Network and go to a particular information area. (Not available in Favorite Places.)
Add to Favorite Places	Adds selected item to Favorite Places. (Not available in Favorite Places.)
Properties	Shows properties of selected item. General properties may include: • Name and Go word • Category, Type, Rating • Price and Description Context properties include: • Language, Topics, People and Place • Forum manager, Owner • Created, Last changed, Size
Up One Level	Opens folder one level higher than current folder.
Sign In	Lets you sign in to MSN.
Sign Out	Lets you sign out of MSN.
Close	Closes the current window without signing you out of MSN.

Continued ...

The Microsoft Network (continued)

Edit	
Cut	Removes selected text and places it in the Clipboard.
Copy	Copies selected text and places it in the Clipboard.
Paste	Inserts contents of Clipboard into current workspace.
Select All	Selects all text in current workspace.
Invert Selection	Deselects selected items and selects previously unselected items.
Go to	Lets you go to the following sections: MSN Central Favorite Places Other Location — Type a Go word for desired service.

View	
Options...	Lets you set properties for folder. General properties include: • Disconnect after *n* minutes of inactivity. • Show MSN Today title on startup. • Content view (language) • Include foreign language content *NOTE: Other property tabs are common to all folders and are not covered here.*

NOTE: Other View menu options are common to all folders and are not covered here.

Continued ...

The Microsoft Network (continued)

Tools	
Find	Lets you find items in one of the following locations: • Files or Folders • Computer • On The Microsoft Network
Password...	Lets you change your MSN password.
Billing	Lets you view or change options in one of the following billing categories: • Payment Method • Summary of Charges • Subscriptions
File Transfer Status	Lets you view and manage files in File Transfer Status window.
Connection Settings...	Lets you view or change settings in one of the following connection categories: • Access Numbers • Dialing Properties • Modem Settings

Volume Control

Lets you control the audio volume for playback, recording and other installed audio devices.

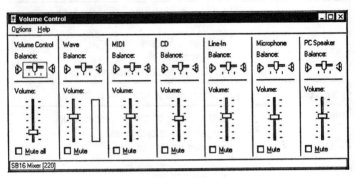

Volume Control Window

Location   **Start** Programs, Accessories, Multimedia
OR
Double-click 🔊 when it appears on taskbar.

*NOTE: If you did not install **The Microsoft Network**, see
Add or Remove Windows Components, page 91.*

What You Can Do with Volume Control

- Quickly open it by double-clicking the speaker icon when it appears on the taskbar.
- Control volume on installed sound devices.
- Control the balance between speakers on installed sound devices.
- Add and remove controls for audio devices.
- Mute one device while playing another to avoid mixing sounds.
- Quickly control the volume from the taskbar.
- Mute all sound devices.

Volume Control (continued)

Volume Control Audio Controls
The illustration below identifies Volume Control's audio controls.

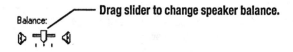

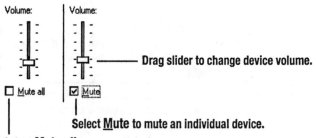

Drag slider to change speaker balance.

Drag slider to change device volume.

Select <u>M</u>ute to mute an individual device.

Select <u>M</u>ute all to mute all devices.

Control Volume Quickly

1 Click . . . .
on taskbar.
A volume control appears above the taskbar.

2 Drag slider up or down.

OR

Select . . . . □ <u>M</u>ute

Volume Control (continued)

Volume Control Menu Commands

Options	
Properties	Lets you set the following properties: • Mixer device Adjust volume for • Playback • Recording • Other • Show the following volume controls: Volume Control, Wave, MIDI, CD, Line-in, Microphone, PC Speaker...
Advanced Controls	Adds an Advanced button to the Volume Control window. You can click this button to set: Tone Controls • Base (Low/High) • Treble (Low/High)
Exit	Exits the Volume Control program.

WordPad

Lets you create, edit, format and print text documents.

WordPad

Location [Start] Programs, Accessories

NOTE: If you did not install WordPad, see Add or Remove Windows Components, page 91.

What You Can Do with WordPad

- Enter and edit text.
- Cut, copy and paste data to and from the Clipboard.
- Save and open text document in Word 6, Rich Text, and Text Only formats.
- Insert, size and move graphics.
- Apply page format commands, including font selection, bulleted lists, paragraph alignment, page breaks, spacing, margins, tabs, indents, headers and footers.
- Print documents.
- Insert embedded or linked OLE objects.

WordPad (continued)

WordPad Toolbar

The illustration below identifies the buttons on WordPad's toolbar.

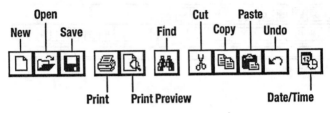

WordPad Format Bar

The illustration below identifies the buttons and controls on WordPad's format bar.

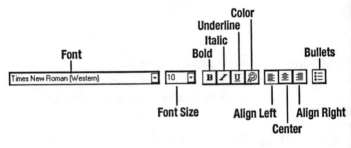

WordPad Ruler

The illustration below identifies the controls on WordPad's ruler.

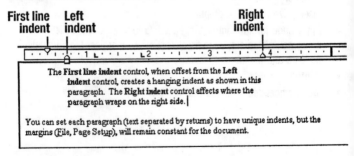

The **First line indent** control, when offset from the **Left indent** control, creates a hanging indent as shown in this paragraph. The **Right indent** control affects where the paragraph wraps on the right side.

You can set each paragraph (text separated by returns) to have unique indents, but the margins (File, Page Setup), will remain constant for the document.

WordPad (continued)

WordPad Menu Commands

File	
New...	Starts new file as one of the following types: Word 6 Document, Rich Text Document, Text Only Document.
Open...	Lets you open a file of the following types: Word for Windows 6.0 (*.doc), Windows Write (*.wri), Rich Text Format (*.rtf), Text Documents (*.txt), Text Documents - MS-DOS Format (*.txt).
Save	Saves document with current name.
Save As...	Lets you save and name current document.
Print...	Lets you print current document and set the following options: Printer • Name • Properties Print range • All, Pages from *n* to *n*, Selection Copies • Number of copies • Collate
Print Preview	Displays how document will look when printed.
Page Setup...	Lets you set the following page options: Paper • Size, Source Orientation • Portrait, Landscape Margins (inches) • Left, Right, Top, Bottom • Printer (set for document)
Send...	Lets you fax or mail current document. (Requires Microsoft Exchange.)
Exit	Exits WordPad program.

Continued ...

WordPad (continued)

Edit	
Undo	Lets you undo your last action.
Cut	Moves selected data to the Clipboard.
Copy	Copies selected data to the Clipboard.
Paste	Inserts data stored in the Clipboard into current document.
Paste Special...	Inserts data stored in the Clipboard into current document and provides the following paste options: • As (select data format) • Paste • Paste Link • Display As Icon
Clear	Deletes selected data.
Select All	Selects all data in document.
Find...	Lets you find specified text in document.
Find Next	Finds next instance of previous search.
Replace...	Lets you find and replace specified text in document.
Links...	Lets you edit link to selected linked object.
Object Properties	Lets you view and set properites of selected object.
Object	Lets you edit selected embedded or linked object.

Continued ..

WordPad (continued)

View	
Toolbar	Shows or hides toolbar.
Format Bar	Shows or hides format bar.
Ruler	Shows or hides ruler.
Status Bar	Shows or hides status bar.
Options...	Lets you set the following options: Options settings include: Measurement units • Inches, Centimeters, Points, Picas • Automatic word selection Text Rich Text, Word 6, Write and Embedded settings include: Word wrap • No wrap, Wrap to window, Wrap to ruler Toolbars • Toolbar, Format bar, Ruler, Status bar

Insert	
Date and Time...	Inserts date and time in document.
Object...	Inserts OLE object in document.

Format	
Font...	Lets you set font for selected text or base font.
Bullet Style	Turns bullet style on or off for current paragraph.
Paragraph...	Lets you set indent and alignment style for paragraph: Indentation • Left, Right, First line • Alignment (Left, Right, Center)
Tabs...	Lets you set or clear tab stops for current paragraph.

In most cases, the noun is the primary key.
For example, look up "File, copy" instead of "Copy file."

In most cases, the noun is the primary key.
For example, look up "File, copy" instead of "Copy file."

270 INDEX

*In most cases, the noun is the primary key.
For example, look up "File, copy" instead of "Copy file."*

In most cases, the noun is the primary key.
For example, look up "File, copy" instead of "Copy file."

In most cases, the noun is the primary key.
For example, look up "File, copy" instead of "Copy file."

In most cases, the noun is the primary key.
For example, look up "File, copy" instead of "Copy file."

In most cases, the noun is the primary key.
For example, look up "File, copy" instead of "Copy file."

In most cases, the noun is the primary key.
For example, look up "File, copy" instead of "Copy file."

In most cases, the noun is the primary key.
For example, look up "File, copy" instead of "Copy file."

In most cases, the noun is the primary key.
For example, look up "File, copy" instead of "Copy file."

In most cases, the noun is the primary key.
For example, look up "File, copy" instead of "Copy file."

In most cases, the noun is the primary key.
For example, look up "File, copy" instead of "Copy file."

In most cases, the noun is the primary key.
For example, look up "File, copy" instead of "Copy file."